ENJOY THE BOOK, AND HAPPY GAMING!

L B BOOKS

Published 2025. Little Brother Books Ltd, 23 Southernhay East, Exeter, Devon, EX11QL

books@littlebrotherbooks.co.uk
www.littlebrotherbooks.co.uk

Printed in Italy.
Little Brother Books, 77 Camden Street Lower, Dublin D02 XE80

The Little Brother Books trademarks, logos, email and website addresses and the GamesWarrior logo and imprint are sole and exclusive properties of Little Brother Books Limited.

HOW TO STAY SAFE IN ROBLOX

Roblox is an exciting world full of games and adventures, and it's a great place to make new friends and learn new skills. But while you're busy having fun, it's really important to remember how to stay safe online. Luckily we've been playing Roblox for years, so here are some of the ways that we think you can enjoy Roblox without any worries.

KEEP YOUR PERSONAL INFORMATION PRIVATE

We think that one of the most important rules in Roblox is to keep your personal details a secret. Never share your full name, address, phone number, school name, or any other personal information with anyone online. Remember, if someone asks for this information, it is best not to give it out. Keeping your private details private helps to stop strangers from knowing too much about you.

BE CAREFUL WITH CHATTING

Roblox has chat features so you can talk with your friends, but we advise that you should always be careful when chatting with others. Always use the safe chat settings that are designed to protect you from inappropriate messages. If someone sends you a message that makes you feel uncomfortable or upset, don't reply. Instead, tell a parent or grown-up right away and use the block feature to stop that person from contacting you again.

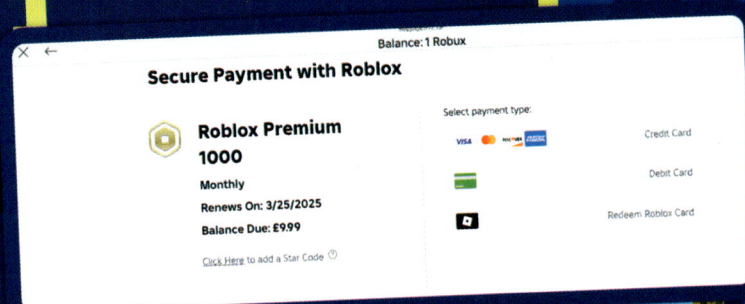

USE PARENTAL CONTROLS AND PRIVACY SETTINGS

Did you know that Roblox has special settings to help keep you safe? We think it's a good idea to ask your parents or another adult you trust to help you set up your account so that only your friends can message you or join your games. You can also set your account to private, which means that only people you know can see what you are doing. Using these controls makes it easier to avoid unwanted visitors in your virtual world.

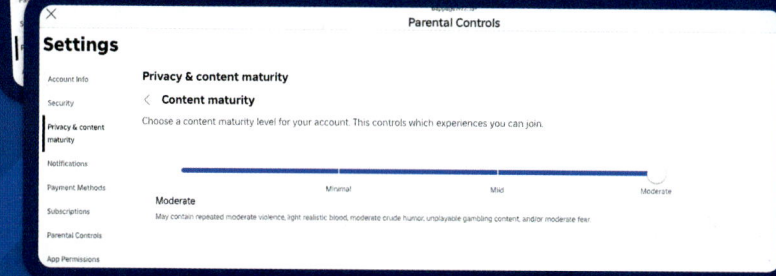

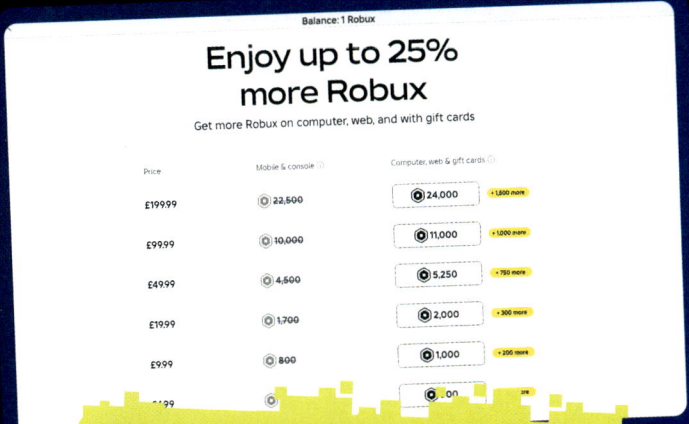

Enjoy up to 25% more Robux

Get more Robux on computer, web, and with gift cards

Price	Mobile & console	Computer, web & gift cards	
£199.99	22,500	24,000	+ 1,500 more
£99.99	10,000	11,000	+ 1,000 more
£49.99	4,500	5,250	+ 750 more
£19.99	1,700	2,000	+ 300 more
£9.99	800	1,000	+ 200 more

REPORT AND BLOCK ANYONE WHO'S NOT NICE

If you ever see someone breaking the rules or being mean in Roblox, we say you should report them. Roblox has a simple way to report bad behaviour and it helps keep the game fun for everyone. You can also block players who aren't nice. Always let an adult know if something seems wrong – they are there to help you.

HAVE FUN AND STAY SMART

Above all, remember that playing Roblox should be a fun and safe experience. By following these tips and using the tools available, you can enjoy all the fantastic games and adventures without worry.

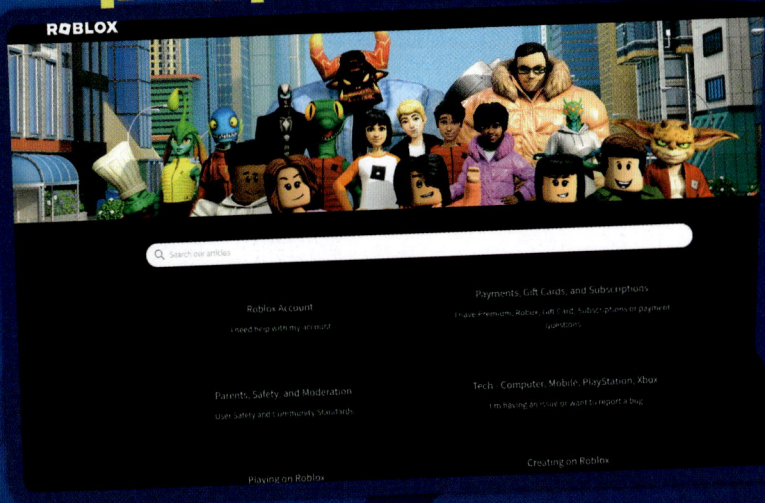

GAMESWARRIOR SAYS

Stay smart, be kind, and always ask for help if you need it. Happy gaming!

PUZZLE CORNER

ROBLOX CROSSWORD CHALLENGE!

Think you know everything about Roblox? Put your skills to the test with this fabulous crossword! From in-game features to popular games, this puzzle is packed with all things Roblox. Whether you're a pro builder, a master trader, or just love exploring new worlds, these clues will challenge your knowledge.

Grab a pencil (or a friend to help!) and see if you can complete the crossword. Good luck, and may the blocks be ever in your favour!

ACROSS

5. A fun obstacle course challenge in Roblox (4)
7. The virtual currency used in Roblox (5)
8. A tool that censors inappropriate words in chat (6)
10. Roblox is a type of video ____ (4)
13. The system used to exchange items with other players (5)
15. The tool used to create and develop games in Roblox (6)
16. What you can do to stop a player from contacting you (5)

DOWN

1. A game where you can build houses and live in a virtual town (8)
2. A paid membership that gives you extra perks (7)
3. A hugely popular Roblox game about raising pets (6,2)
6. People you add to play and chat with in Roblox (7)
9. Someone who creates games on Roblox (9)
11. Your character that represents you in the game (6)
12. A community players can join to chat and work together (5)
14. What you should do if you see someone breaking the rules (6)

ANSWERS ON PAGE 77.

ROBLOX WORDSEARCH CHALLENGE!

Get ready for a Roblox-themed word hunt! Hidden in this puzzle are words related to your favourite games, features, and adventures in Roblox. Some words are easy to spot, while others are cleverly hidden – can you find them all?

Grab a pencil and start searching! Challenge yourself or race against a friend to see who can complete it first. Have fun, and happy hunting!

P	D	O	G	R	U	B	X	O	L	B	R	V	C
U	E	A	B	I	N	V	E	N	T	O	R	Y	C
O	B	V	P	B	V	P	A	R	K	O	U	R	N
R	M	A	R	R	Y	T	Y	C	O	O	N	U	W
N	A	T	R	N	P	O	R	U	M	E	N	G	A
N	R	A	R	B	F	U	W	U	M	M	O	G	P
O	K	R	E	O	S	T	I	T	R	S	T	T	S
I	E	O	U	A	M	M	P	S	T	U	D	I	O
Y	T	O	U	O	E	O	T	A	N	D	O	X	D
O	P	M	K	R	D	R	E	O	R	Y	N	T	B
L	L	B	P	A	O	O	T	G	Y	O	R	M	M
U	A	A	U	L	O	B	A	G	D	A	L	U	I
N	C	L	D	G	D	U	C	V	L	A	P	B	R
P	E	A	I	P	R	X	R	E	C	T	B	W	P

WORDS

- [ ] ROBUX
- [ ] BLOXBURG
- [ ] STUDIO
- [ ] PARKOUR
- [ ] AVATAR
- [ ] SPAWN
- [ ] ADOPT ME
- [ ] BADGE
- [ ] TYCOON
- [ ] OBBY
- [ ] PREMIUM
- [ ] INVENTORY
- [ ] MARKETPLACE

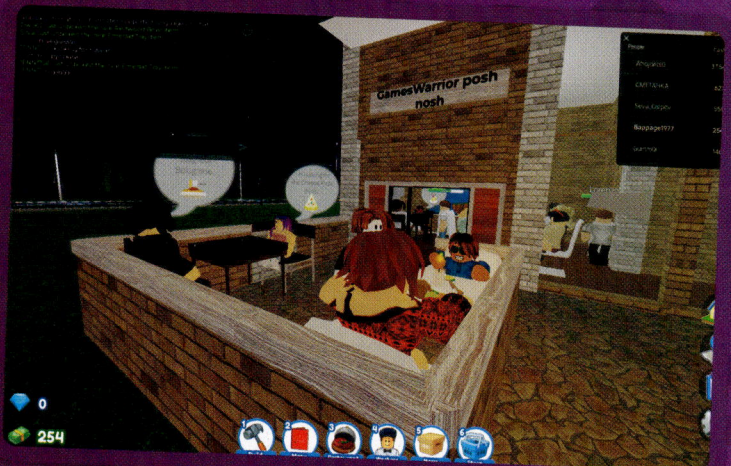

ANSWERS ON PAGE 77.

TEN AMAZING ROBLOX FACTS!

Ready to learn some awesome facts about your favourite gaming world? Whether you're new to Roblox or a seasoned player, these fun facts are sure to amaze you! Here are ten of our favourite Roblox facts – how many did you know?

1. ROBLOX IS OLDER THAN YOU THINK!

Roblox was launched way back in 2006. That's almost ancient in gaming years! Its founders were David Baszucki and Erik Cassel who have become mega rich thanks to Roblox's success!

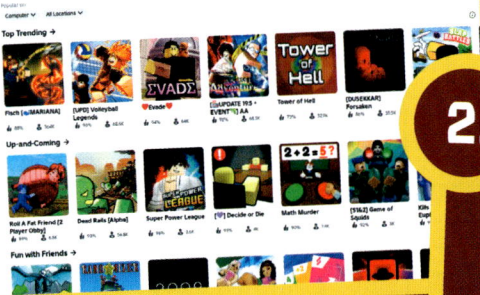

2. MILLIONS OF GAMES TO PLAY

There are over 40 million games on Roblox and they're all created by players like you. From obstacle courses to pet simulators, there's something for everyone.

3. A MASSIVE COMMUNITY

Roblox has more than 380 million active users every month. That's like the whole population of the UK – three times over!

4. YOU CAN BE A GAME DEVELOPER

On Roblox, anyone can create a game. All you need is Roblox Studio (which is free!) and a great idea. Who knows? You could design the next big hit!

5. ROBUX GALORE

Every day, players spend millions of Robux in the Roblox Marketplace. It's one of the busiest virtual shopping centres in the world.

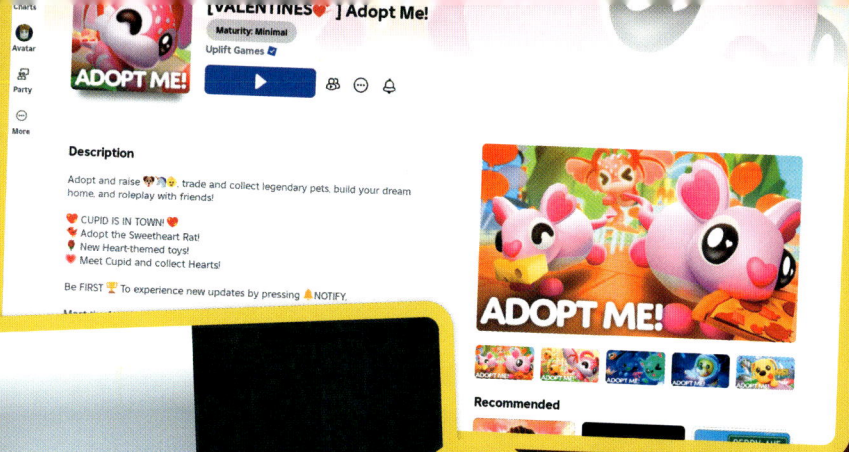

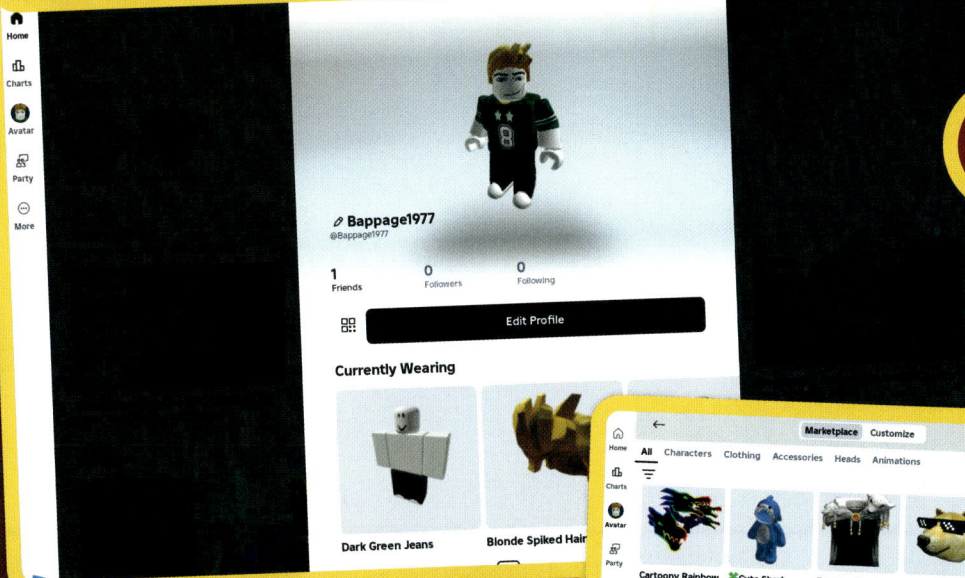

6. AVATARS HAVE ENDLESS STYLE

There are billions of ways to customise your avatar. From funky hats to superhero capes, your imagination is the only limit!

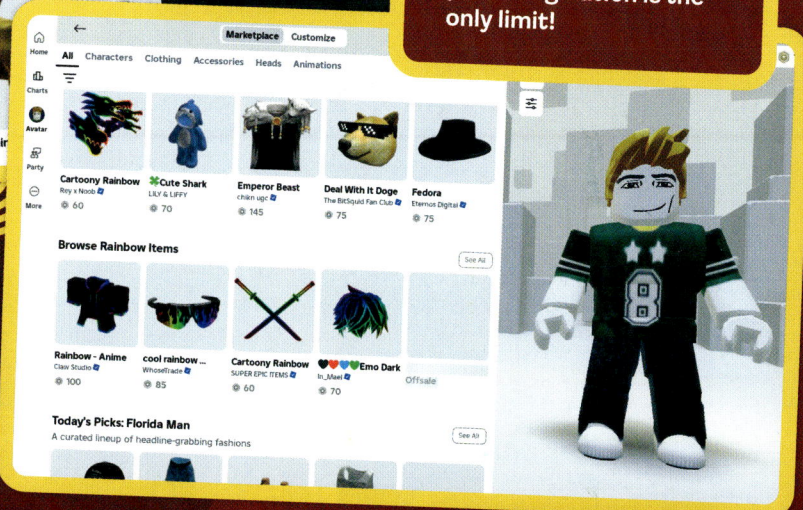

7. REAL-WORLD SKILLS

Playing and creating on Roblox teaches skills like problem-solving, coding and even teamwork. It's learning disguised as fun!

8. GLOBAL FUN

Roblox is played in over 180 countries. Wherever you go, there's always someone ready to play.

9. RECORD BREAKERS!

One of the most popular games on Roblox, Adopt Me!, once hit over 1.9 million players online at the same time – a world record for the platform!

10. VIRTUAL WORLD

Roblox isn't just about games. It's also a growing virtual world where people hang out, attend concerts and even celebrate birthdays!

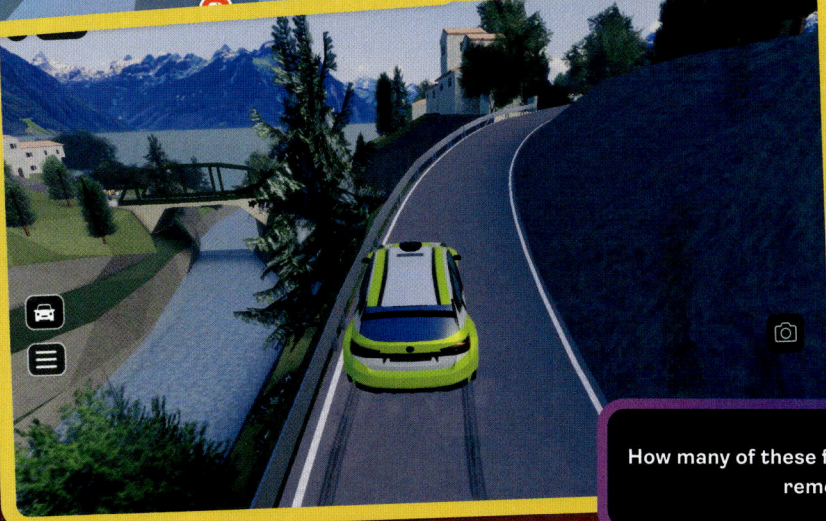

GAMESWARRIOR SAYS

How many of these facts did you already know? Next time you play Roblox, remember – you're part of something epic!

ARE YOU A ROBLOX EXPERT?

Welcome, quiz whiz! Get ready to put your thinking cap on and have a bit of fun with our quiz packed with ten brilliant questions. It's a quick adventure for your brain, so grab a biscuit, relax and see how many you can answer. Good luck and enjoy the challenge!

1 WHO ARE THE TWO GENIUS GAMES DESIGNERS THAT CREATED ROBLOX?

2 WHAT YEAR WAS ROBLOX LAUNCHED?

3 WHAT IS THE MOST IMMERSIVE WAY TO PLAY?

4 WHAT IS AN 'OBBY' IN ROBLOX?

5 WHERE ARE AVATARS CUSTOMISED?

6 WHAT NAME IS GIVEN TO ROBLOX GAMES THAT LET YOU BUILD A BUSINESS?

DIVE INTO ROBLOX WITH VR!

Alright, you brilliant builders and adventurous explorers! Have you ever dreamed of stepping inside your favourite Roblox worlds? Well, grab your virtual reality (VR) goggles, because now you can! Imagine building your dream house, battling dragons, or racing supercars; all while feeling like you're actually there. That's the magic of Roblox in VR!

ROBLOX IN VR: A WHOLE NEW WORLD!

Roblox is already awesome, but we think that playing it in VR makes it even more exciting. You can explore your favourite games in a whole new way. Imagine walking through the spooky hallways of a horror game, or flying high above a city in a superhero simulator. It's a totally immersive experience, and we love it!

WHAT'S VR ANYWAY?

Think of VR as a super-powered pair of goggles that take you to a completely different place. When you put on a VR headset, you see a 3D world all around you. You can move your head to look around, and sometimes, you can even use special controllers to interact with things in the game. It's like stepping into a movie, but you get to be the star!

AWESOME ROBLOX VR GAMES TO TRY:

- **Natural Disaster Survival:** Feel the rumble of earthquakes and the splash of floods as you try to survive a range of crazy disasters. We think you'll find it's much more thrilling when you feel like you're really there!

- **VR Hands:** This game is great because you can play with non-VR friends - you control a huge pair of hands and must help your friends negotiate an obstacle course by covering obstacles and helping them to progress!

- **Cook Burgers:** Ever wanted to flip burgers in a busy restaurant? In VR, you can! We found it fun to try and keep up with all the orders, and it made us feel like a real chef.

- **Robloxian High School:** Go to school, meet friends, and explore the hallways in VR. We think this is a great way to socialise and have fun in a virtual world.

WHICH HEADSET IS RIGHT FOR YOU?

To play Roblox in VR, you'll need a compatible headset. Here are a couple of popular options that we've tested for ourselves and recommend:

- **Meta Quest 2/Meta Quest 3:** These are wireless headsets, which means you don't need to be plugged into a computer. They're easy to set up, and we think they offer a great VR experience.

- **PC VR headsets (like the Valve Index or HTC Vive):** If you have a powerful gaming computer, you can use these headsets. They often offer higher-quality graphics and more advanced features. However, they are generally more expensive and we found that they need a more complex setup.

IMPORTANT GAMESWARRIOR RECOMMENDATIONS!

- Always ask a grown-up before using a VR headset.

- Take breaks! VR can be tiring, so don't play for too long at once.

- Make sure you have plenty of space to move around safely.

- Be careful of the cables if using a wired headset.

So, are you ready to jump into the world of Roblox VR? Get your headset on, and get ready for an adventure like no other!

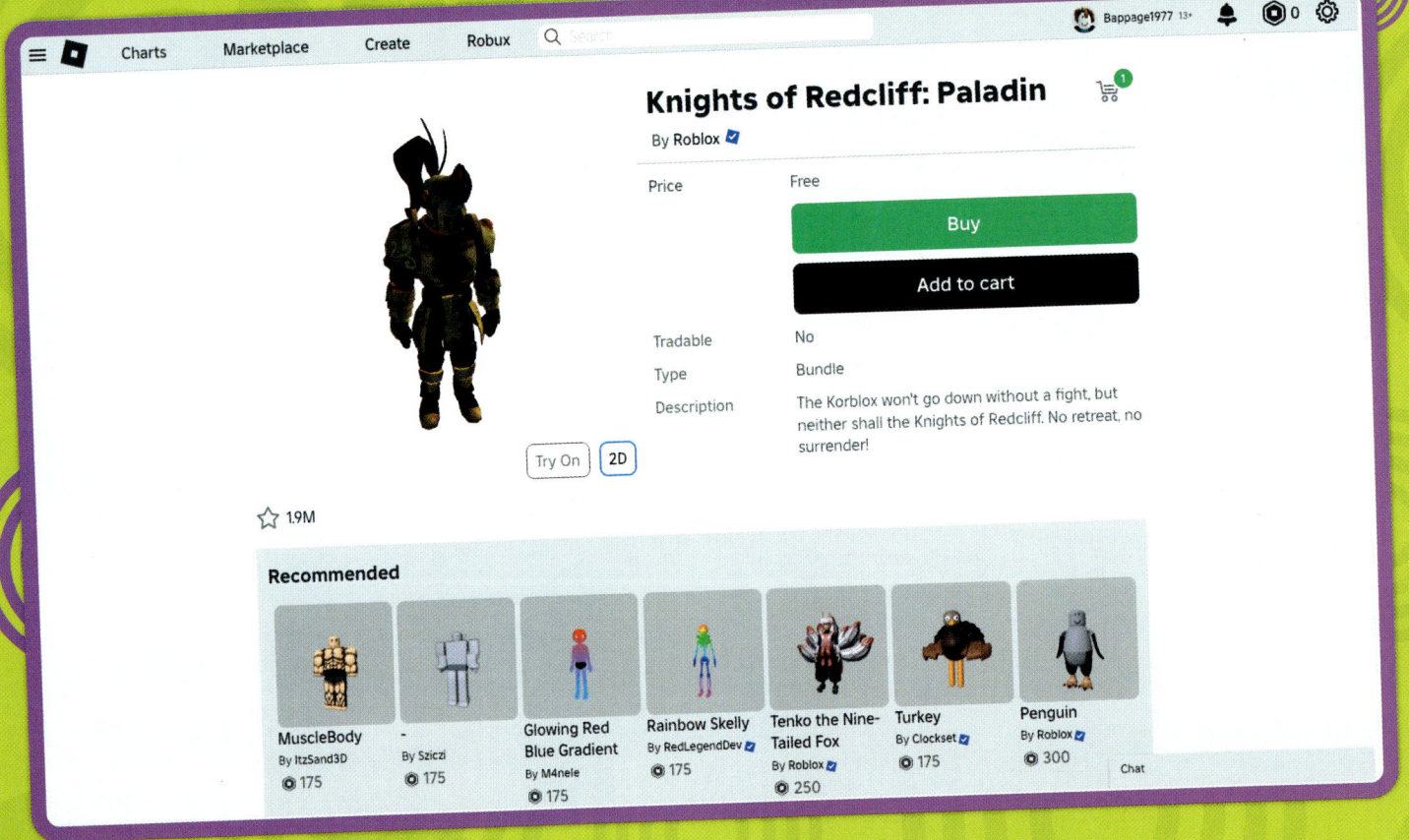

ROBUX AND THE MARKETPLACE:
YOUR GUIDE

Welcome to the world of Roblox! If you've ever wanted to know all about Robux and how the Roblox Marketplace works, you're in the right place. Let's dive in!

WHAT ARE ROBUX?

Robux is the special currency used in Roblox. Think of it as the money that lets you buy cool stuff in the game. Want awesome outfits, unique gear, or exclusive access to games? Robux is the key!

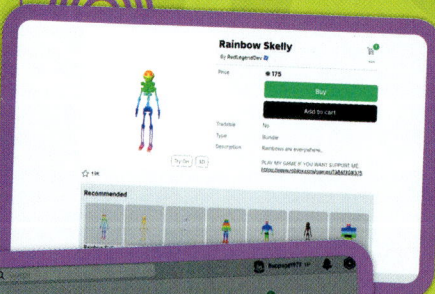

HOW DO YOU GET ROBUX?

There are a few ways to get your hands on Robux.

1. **Buy Robux:** You can purchase them using real money. Always ask a parent or guardian first!

2. **Roblox Premium:** This is a monthly subscription that gives you a set amount of Robux each month, plus other perks.

3. **Earn Robux:** If you're a game developer on Roblox, you can earn Robux when people play your games or buy items you've created.

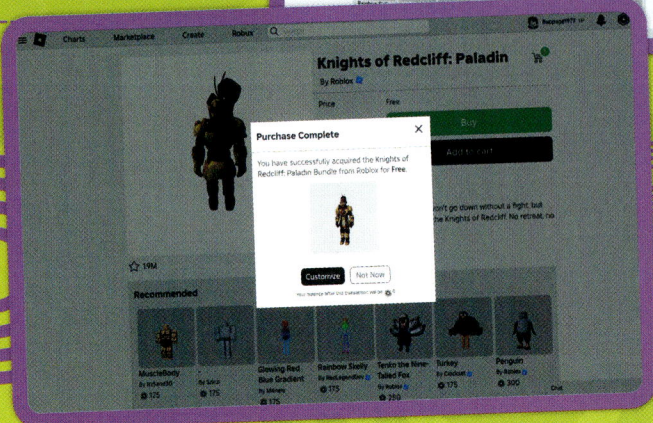

SPENDING ROBUX

Here's where the fun begins! You can spend your Robux on:

- **Clothes and Accessories:** Style your avatar with outfits, hats, shoes, and more.

- **Game Passes:** These are special perks in games, like faster cars or superpowers!

- **Items and Upgrades:** Buy cool tools, weapons, or pets for your adventures.

Be sure to spend your Robux wisely – once they're gone, they're gone!

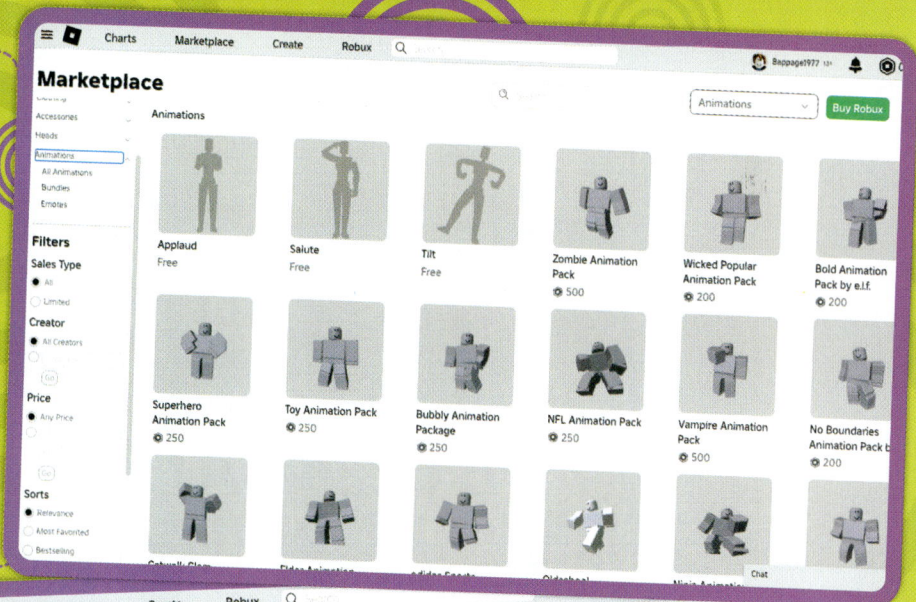

Enjoy up to 25% more Robux

Get more Robux on computer, web, and with gift cards

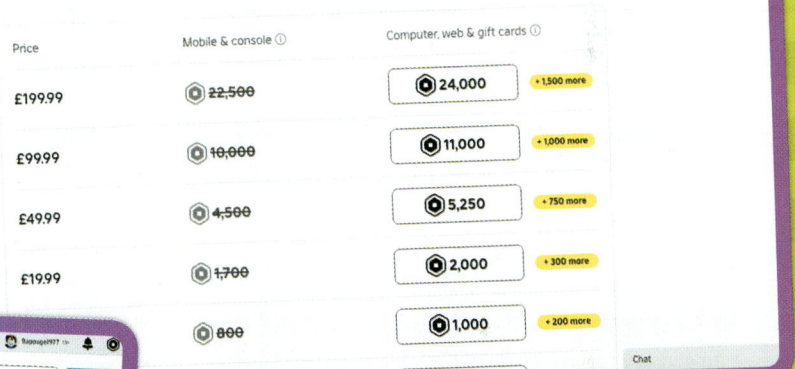

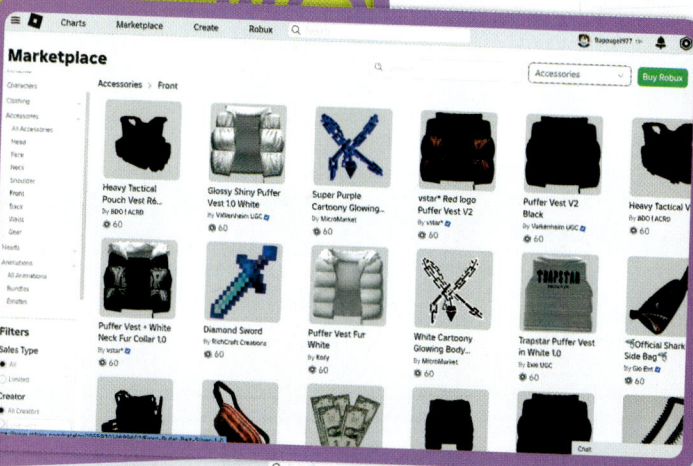

Price	Mobile & console ⓘ	Computer, web & gift cards ⓘ	
£199.99	⬢ 22,500	⬢ 24,000	+ 1,500 more
£99.99	⬢ 10,000	⬢ 11,000	+ 1,000 more
£49.99	⬢ 4,500	⬢ 5,250	+ 750 more
£19.99	⬢ 1,700	⬢ 2,000	+ 300 more
	⬢ 800	⬢ 1,000	+ 200 more

WHAT IS THE ROBLOX MARKETPLACE?

The Marketplace is like a giant online shop where players can buy and sell items. Here's how it works:

- **Buying:** Browse through thousands of creations made by other players.

- **Selling:** If you've designed a cool shirt or a useful item, you can sell it for Robux!

- **Trading:** Players can also trade items, but remember to be careful and only trade with people you trust.

GAMES WARRIOR SAYS

We think that Robux makes Roblox even more enjoyable by letting you customise your experience and stand out from the crowd. Whether you're designing your dream outfit, creating a hit game, or buying power-ups, Robux opens up a world of possibilities – but remember, with so many free experiences out there, you don't have to spend a fortune to get lots out of your Roblox experience.

GET READY TO STYLE UP!

THE ULTIMATE GUIDE TO CUSTOMISING YOUR ROBLOX AVATAR

Hey there, Roblox fans! Have you ever wanted to stand out in a sea of blocky characters, looking cooler than a penguin wearing sunglasses? Well, you're in luck! Roblox is not just about playing games – it's also about expressing yourself. Whether you want to look like a medieval knight, a futuristic robot, or just a really fancy cat, there are loads of ways to customise your avatar. And the best part? You can do it for free – or go all out with Robux if you're feeling fancy!

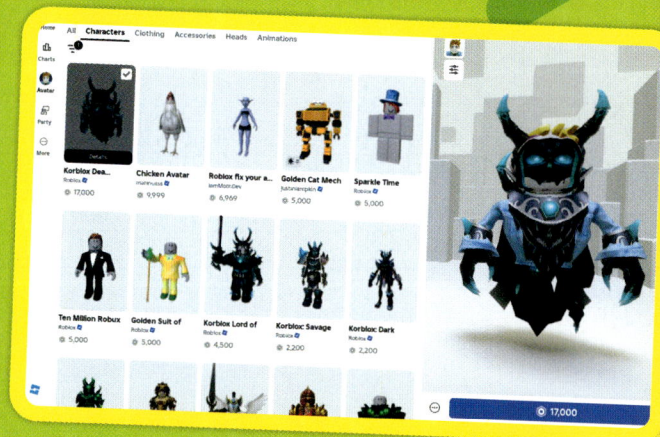

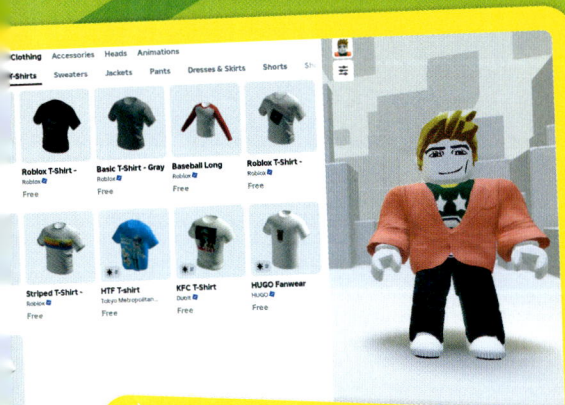

FREE CUSTOMISATION

BECAUSE LOOKING COOL SHOULDN'T COST A PENNY

Let's start with the best kind of customisation: the FREE kind! When you first create a Roblox account, you're given a default avatar, but that's just the beginning. Head over to the Avatar Editor (found in the menu) and start experimenting. Here are some ways you can customise without spending a single Robux:

- **Clothing and accessories:** Roblox provides a bunch of free shirts, trousers, and accessories in the Avatar Shop. If you dig around, you'll find some real gems!

- **Body shapes and faces:** Want a new face? No problem! Roblox offers free face styles, and you can even adjust your avatar's body shape.

- **Hair styles:** There are free hair options to suit all styles, from spiky to smooth. Mix and match to get the perfect look!

- **Colour changes:** Change your avatar's skin tone to any colour under the sun – green, blue, purple, even rainbow if you're feeling adventurous!

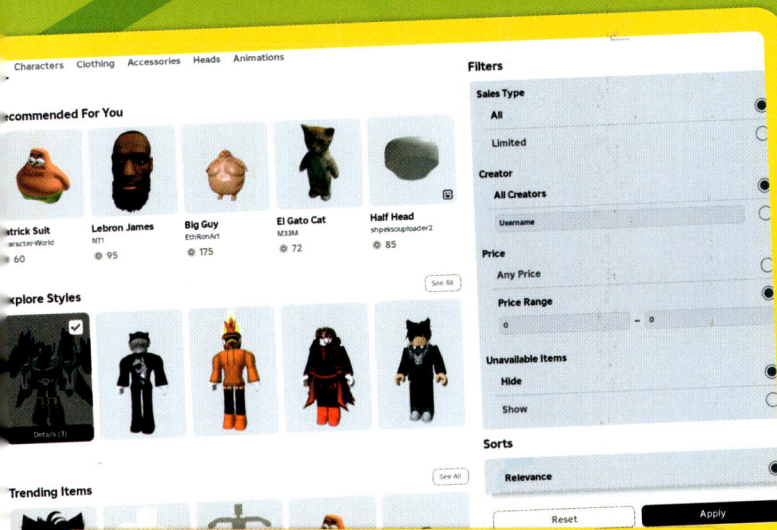

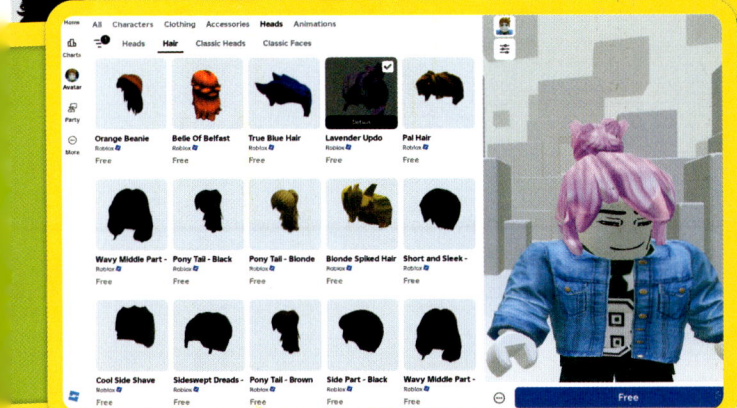

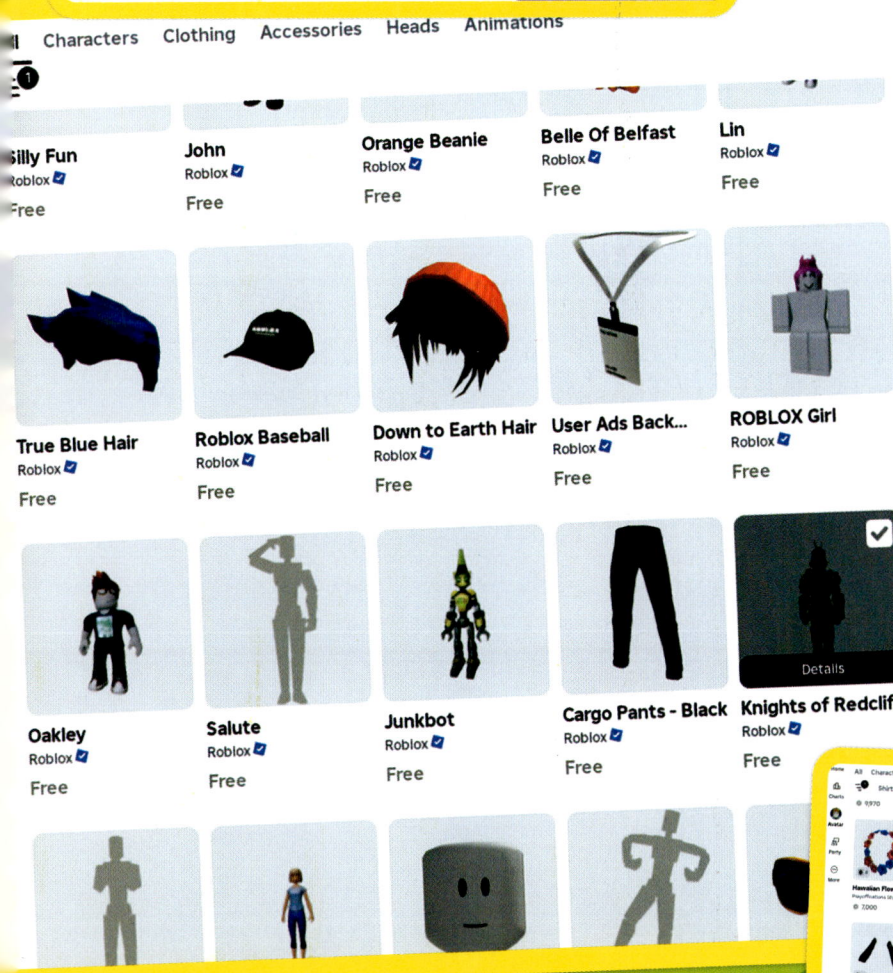

CUSTOMISATION WITH ROBUX

If you're willing to spend some Robux, you can take your avatar customisation to the next level! Here's what you can unlock:

- **Exclusive clothing and accessories:** The Avatar Shop has thousands of designer outfits made by players and official creators. Fancy a golden crown? How about a pizza hat? The choices are endless!

- **Animation packs:** Want to walk like a ninja or jump like a superhero? Animation packs change the way your avatar moves, adding even more personality.

- **Limited edition items:** Some super-rare items are only available for a short time and can even go up in value – like a virtual investment!

- **UGC (user-generated content):** The Roblox community creates incredible custom items, from neon wings to floating ghost companions. If you can dream it, someone's probably made it!

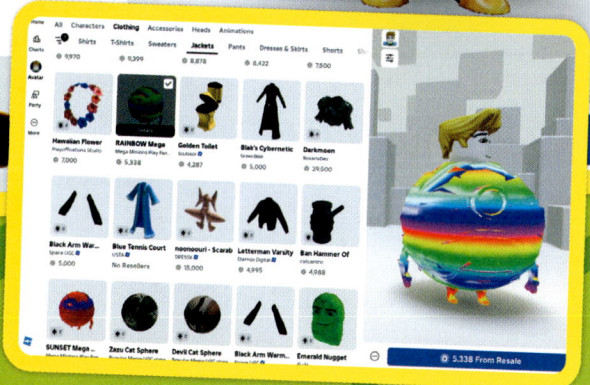

2D Jeff [RECOL...
Aefek
⊚ 175

⊚ 175

IN-GAME OUTFITS

DRESS TO IMPRESS!

Did you know that some Roblox games let you wear special outfits just while you're playing? That's right! You don't always need to spend Robux to rock a new look. Here are some games where you can change outfits just by playing:

- **Brookhaven:** One of the most popular roleplay games, where you can pick from loads of outfits for free. Want to be a superhero? A secret agent? A chef? It's all possible!

- **Tower of Hell:** While it's mostly about climbing impossible towers, sometimes there are limited-time event outfits you can wear.

- **Adopt Me!:** You can dress up not only yourself but also your pets. A unicorn in sunglasses? Yes, please!

- **Royale High:** This game has a huge selection of dresses, wings, and accessories that make you look straight out of a fairy tale.

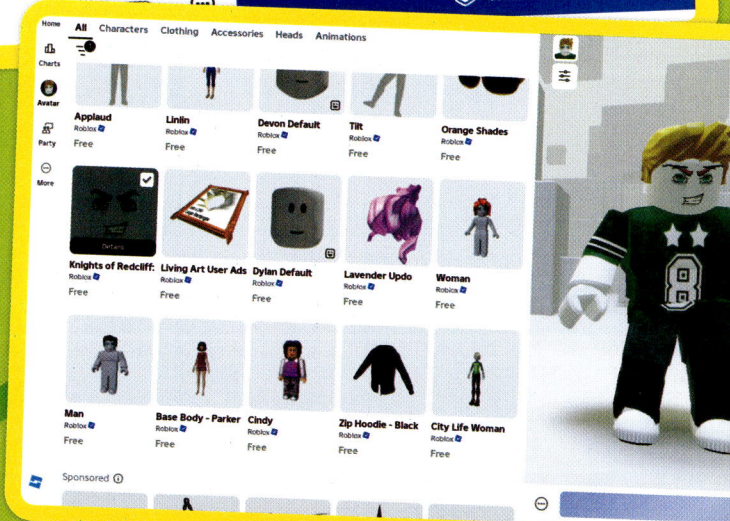

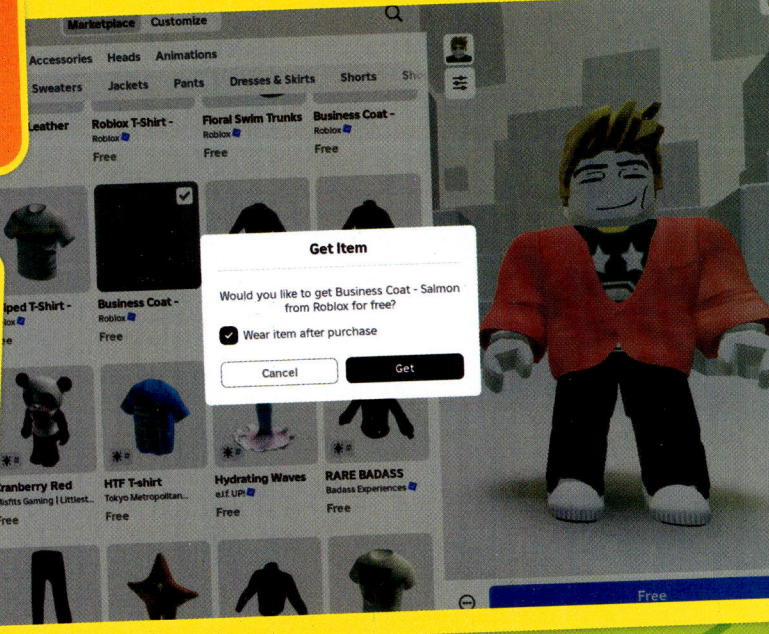

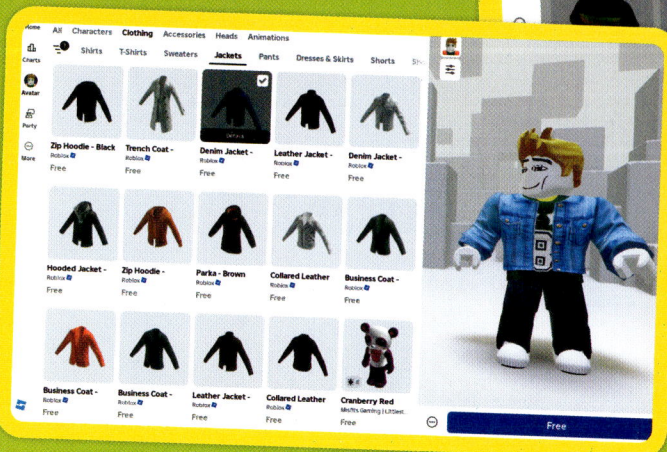

MIX AND MATCH

BE YOUR OWN DESIGNER

One of the best things about customising your Roblox avatar is the freedom to mix and match. You don't have to buy full outfits – grab a cool jacket here, a funky hat there, and create your own signature style. Want to be a pirate with bunny ears? Go for it! A giant banana with a robot arm? Why not?!

Final tips for avatar awesomeness:

1. **Check the Avatar Shop often:** Free items and limited-time offers pop up regularly, so don't miss out!

2. **Try layering your clothing:** Roblox now allows layered clothing, so you can wear a jacket over a t-shirt or a hoodie over a suit!

3. **Follow Roblox creators:** Some developers give out promo codes for free exclusive items.

4. **Have fun!:** At the end of the day, your avatar should represent YOU. Whether you're a fashionista, a warrior, or a blocky alien, make your avatar your own!

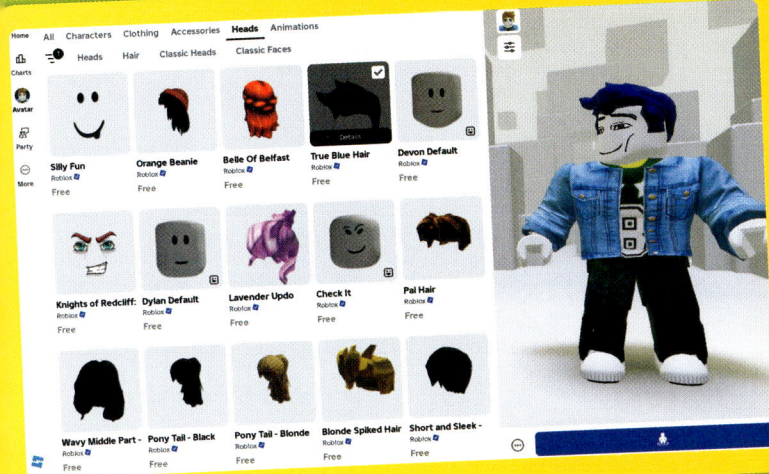

Avatar Refinement

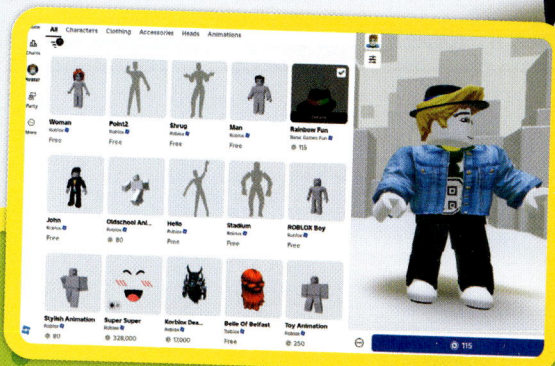

So what are you waiting for? Go and give your Roblox avatar a glow-up – it's time to shine! And remember, the most important thing about customising your avatar is to have fun and let your personality shine through. See you in the game!

PUZZLE GAMES

Roblox is brimming with brilliant puzzle games that challenge your mind while keeping the fun factor sky-high! These games invite you to solve brain-teasers, arrange clever patterns and work out tricky challenges in a colourful and engaging way. Whether you're parking a car just right, matching blocks perfectly, uncovering hidden clues in a cosy cabin, or guessing the mystery word, there's a puzzle adventure waiting for you. Let's explore how these games work, what you do in them, and why they're such a brilliant way to give your brain a little workout!

WHAT DO YOU DO IN PUZZLE GAMES?

In these games, you dive right into the challenge! You might need to manoeuvre a car into a tight space, piece together colourful blocks, explore a mysterious cabin to uncover secrets, or guess a word by using your vocabulary skills. Each game tests a different part of your cleverness, so every session is a new adventure for your mind.

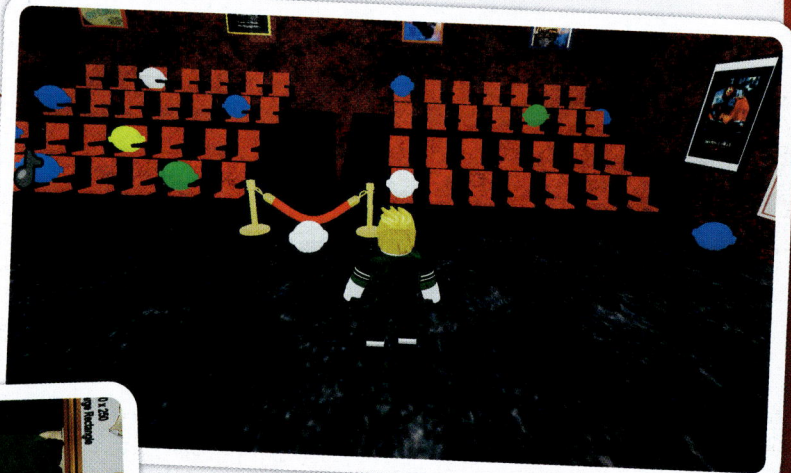

HOW DO PUZZLE GAMES WORK?

Puzzle games on Roblox use simple yet clever challenges that make you think. You're given tasks that might involve arranging objects, solving riddles, or finding hidden clues. These games are designed to be both bright and engaging, often with levels that gradually get trickier as you master each challenge.

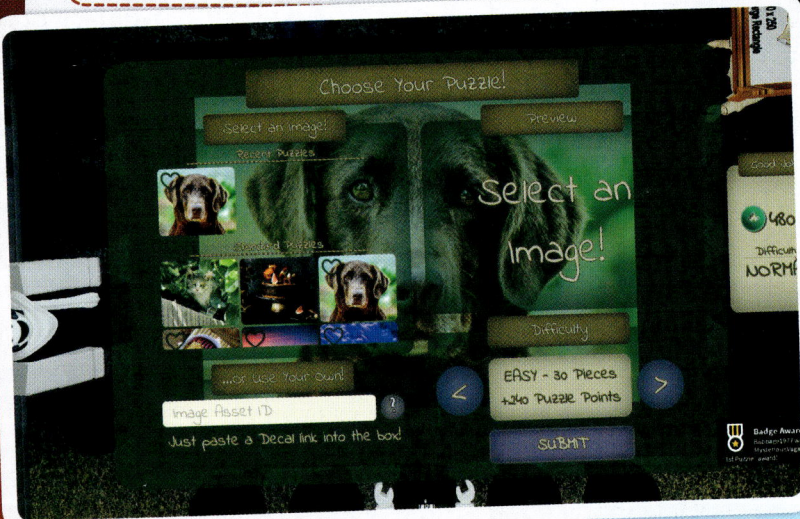

WHY ARE PUZZLE GAMES SO FUN?

The fun of puzzle games lies in their mix of creativity and challenge. They give you the joy of solving problems while enjoying eye-catching designs and playful themes. With each puzzle you crack, there's a great sense of achievement that makes you want to keep playing and try even more clever challenges!

PARKING PANIC

Parking Panic is a Roblox puzzle game that tests your ability to think quickly and plan ahead. In this experience, you're challenged to help the red car out of a seemingly gridlocked car park by moving each vehicle in turn. Sounds simple, doesn't it? Trust us – it's not!

WHY WE LOVE IT

- It combines quick thinking with a fun, practical challenge.

- The difficulty is well-judged and the levels get gradually more challenging.

- Bright colourful cars make it easier to see how you need to move each vehicle.

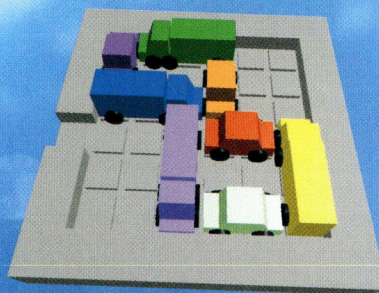

GAMESWARRIOR SAYS

If you get in a real mess, a nice touch is that you can press the 'r' button to start the level with the vehicles in their original position again!

Parking Panic is a delightful puzzle game for anyone who loves a clever challenge. If you enjoy putting your planning skills to the test in a colourful setting, this game is definitely worth a try.

GAMESWARRIOR VERDICT

8/10

BLOCK PUZZLE

Block Puzzle is a fun Roblox game that challenges you to arrange colourful blocks into the right order. It's a bit like Tetris, only you can place your pieces wherever you like. It requires a lot of thinking to complete lines and score points!

WHY WE LOVE IT

- It's a brilliant way to test your logic and problem-solving skills.

- Nice bright colours make the game easy on the eye – and help you to spot patterns.

- The longer you play, the more challenging the game gets!

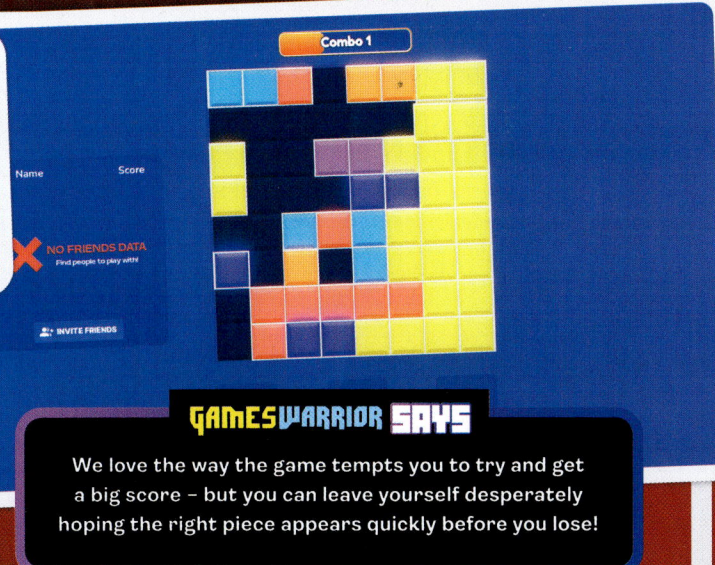

GAMESWARRIOR SAYS

We love the way the game tempts you to try and get a big score – but you can leave yourself desperately hoping the right piece appears quickly before you lose!

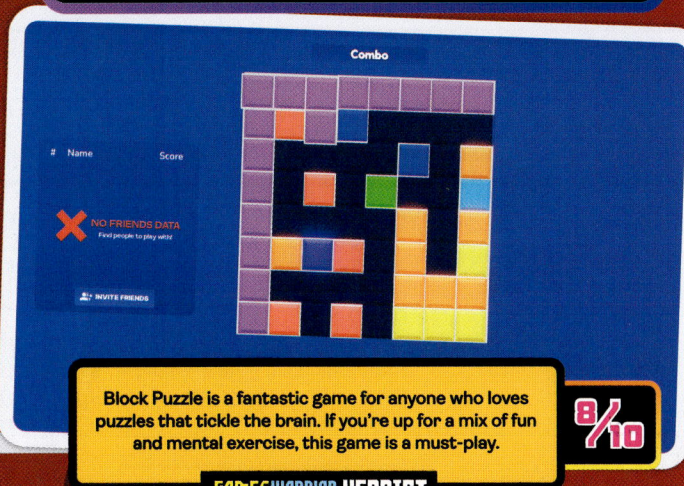

Block Puzzle is a fantastic game for anyone who loves puzzles that tickle the brain. If you're up for a mix of fun and mental exercise, this game is a must-play.

GAMESWARRIOR VERDICT

8/10

PUZZLE CABIN

Puzzle Cabin is a cosy Roblox game that invites you into a charming cabin filled with engaging jigsaw puzzles. You can decide on a difficulty setting from easy to nightmare and just relax as you puzzle away!

WHY WE LOVE IT

- Its cosy, inviting atmosphere makes puzzle-solving feel like a fun adventure.

- The different difficulty settings mean it's entertaining for all ages.

- The detailed cabin setting adds a delightful layer of charm to the experience – with sofas to hang and chat to other puzzle fans.

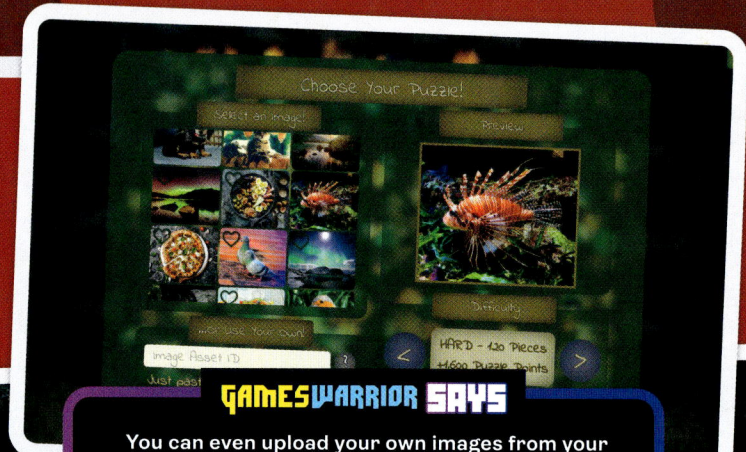

GAMESWARRIOR SAYS
You can even upload your own images from your computer to create jigsaw puzzles all of your own!

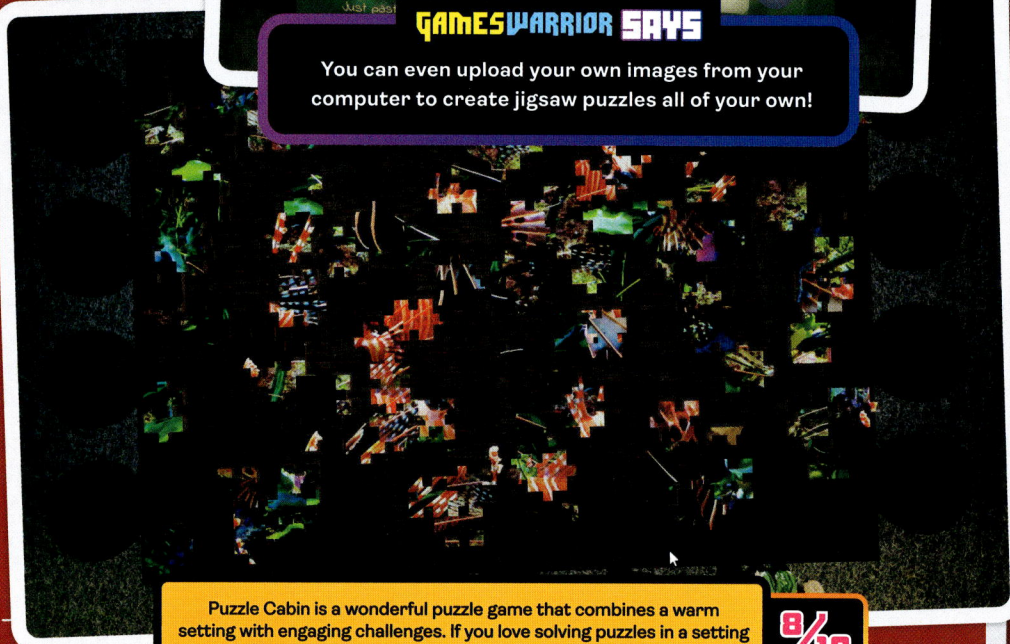

Puzzle Cabin is a wonderful puzzle game that combines a warm setting with engaging challenges. If you love solving puzzles in a setting that feels like a secret hideaway, this game is sure to captivate you.

GAMESWARRIOR VERDICT

8/10

WORDIE

Wordie is a bright and engaging Roblox puzzle game that brings the popular word guessing challenge with a similar name to Roblox. In this experience, you're given a chance to guess a mystery word within a set number of attempts, putting your vocabulary and deduction skills to the test.

WHY WE LOVE IT

- It's a clever and fun way to challenge your word skills.

- The game's design is simple, bright, and easy to understand.

- Each round is a fresh challenge that keeps you thinking and guessing.

GAMESWARRIOR SAYS
You can play different game modes for extra challenges – such as hardcore, with difficult words and only one life. Can you top the leaderboard?

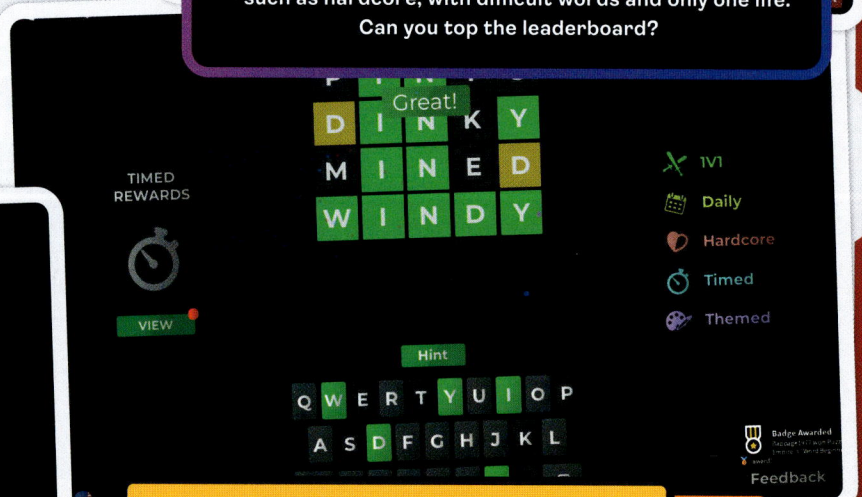

Wordie is an engaging puzzle game for anyone who enjoys testing their vocabulary. If you love a good word challenge, this game is definitely worth a go.

GAMESWARRIOR VERDICT

8/10

A) 2 + 2 =
B) 1 - 0 =
C) 3 X 2 =
D) 6 ÷ 2 =

Solve the questions
Each answer is one digit
Input the digits into the
correct order

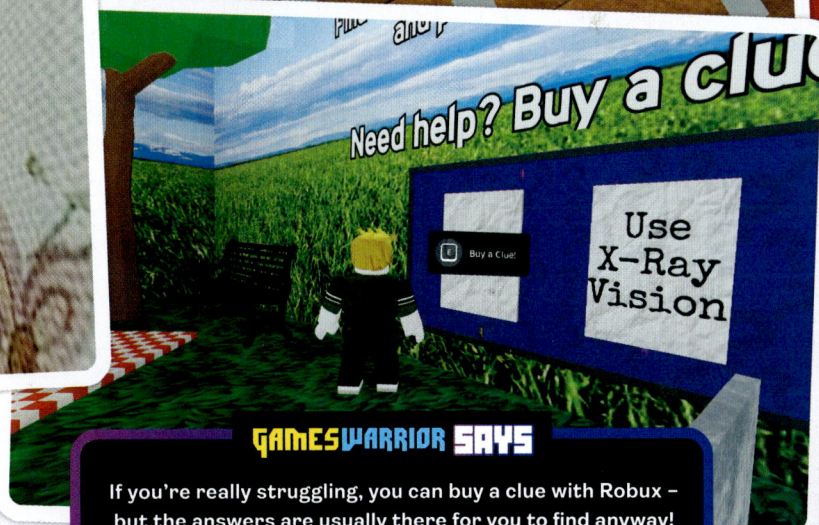

Need help?

Need help? Buy a clue

Use
X-Ray
Vision

Buy a Clue!

ESCAPE ROOM

Escape Room invites you to step into a mysterious room full of challenges. You find yourself locked in a room where your task is to solve a puzzle in order to escape. The game is designed to test your problem-solving skills as you search every nook and cranny for hidden clues and work out clever solutions to unlock the door to freedom.

As you progress through the levels, you encounter a variety of puzzles that require logical thinking, careful observation, and a touch of creativity. Every solved puzzle gives you a burst of excitement, knowing you're one step closer to breaking free. The game encourages you to work through challenges at your own pace, making the journey to escape as rewarding as the victory itself.

GAMESWARRIOR SAYS

If you're really struggling, you can buy a clue with Robux – but the answers are usually there for you to find anyway!

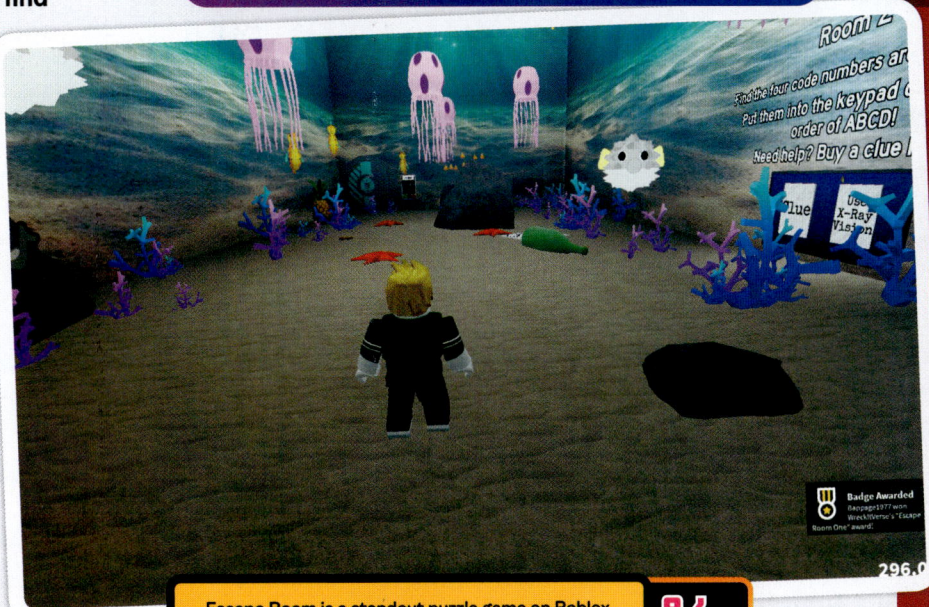

Room 2

Find the four code numbers and
Put them into the keypad in
order of ABCD!
Need help? Buy a clue!

Clue!

Use
X-Ray
Vision

Badge Awarded
6aspge1977 won
WrackWarrior's 'Escape
Room One' award!

296.0

Escape Room is a standout puzzle game on Roblox that brilliantly combines mystery, challenge and fun.

GAMESWARRIOR VERDICT

9/10

OBSTACLE GAMES
(OBBIES)

Roblox is bursting with exciting obstacle games – or 'obbies' as we like to call them – that challenge your balance, speed and quick thinking. These games turn simple parkour into brilliant adventures where every jump, slide and sprint can be a test of skill. Whether you're riding a bike through tricky twists, climbing towering courses, or working together with friends to crack clever puzzles, there's an obby to suit every adventurer. Let's jump into what makes these obstacle challenges exciting and why they're a brilliant way to have a bit of a race against the clock!

WHAT DO YOU DO IN OBSTACLE GAMES?

In these games, you dive straight into a course filled with challenges. You might be balancing on narrow beams, leaping between platforms, or even solving puzzles as you race against time. Some obbies let you work with friends to overcome hurdles, while others challenge you to beat your own best time. Every run is a chance to improve and have a blast!

WHY ARE OBSTACLE GAMES SO FUN?

The thrill of obstacle games lies in the rush of speed, the satisfaction of a well-timed jump, and the reward of overcoming tricky challenges. They mix physical skill with a bit of clever thinking, making every run exciting and full of surprises. With bright designs and a playful spirit; obbies on Roblox are a fantastic way to test your agility and share a laugh with mates.

HOW DO OBSTACLE GAMES WORK?

Obstacle games on Roblox are built around a series of physical challenges that require precision and agility. You're presented with a variety of platforms, moving parts and sometimes even puzzles, all designed to test your timing and coordination. Each level typically gets a bit trickier, so you'll need to stay alert and think on your feet – or on your bike!

OBBY BUT YOU'RE ON A BIKE

Obby But You're On A Bike is a quirky twist on the classic obby challenge, where you must navigate a course while riding a bike. In this experience, you balance and pedal through a series of obstacles, testing your reflexes and coordination in a whole new way.

WHY WE LOVE IT

- It turns the typical obstacle challenge into an exciting cycling adventure.

- The game offers a unique blend of balance and speed that keeps you on your toes.

- Its bright, colourful design makes each ride a joyous experience.

GAMESWARRIOR SAYS

Try practising in the easier sections – mastering the basics on your bike can really help you tackle the trickier parts later on!

Obby But You're On A Bike is a delightful change of pace for anyone who loves a good physical challenge. If you fancy testing your bike riding skills in an obstacle-packed setting, this game is definitely worth a go.

GAMESWARRIOR VERDICT

8/10

TOWER OF HELL

Tower of Hell is a hugely popular obby that challenges you to climb a towering structure filled with tricky platforms and moving obstacles. In this game, every level tests your jumping skills and timing as you race against the clock to reach the top.

WHY WE LOVE IT

- It's a brilliant test of your agility with ever-changing obstacles.

- The challenge of beating your best time makes each run exciting.

- Its simple design ensures that every jump counts in a fun, competitive way.

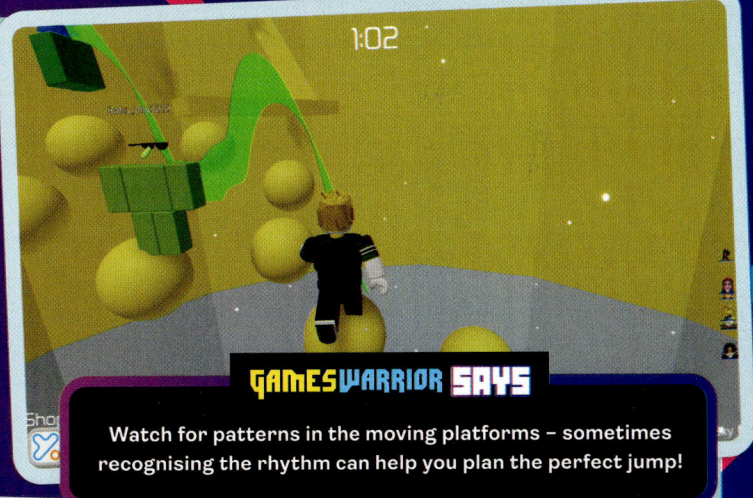

GAMESWARRIOR SAYS

Watch for patterns in the moving platforms – sometimes recognising the rhythm can help you plan the perfect jump!

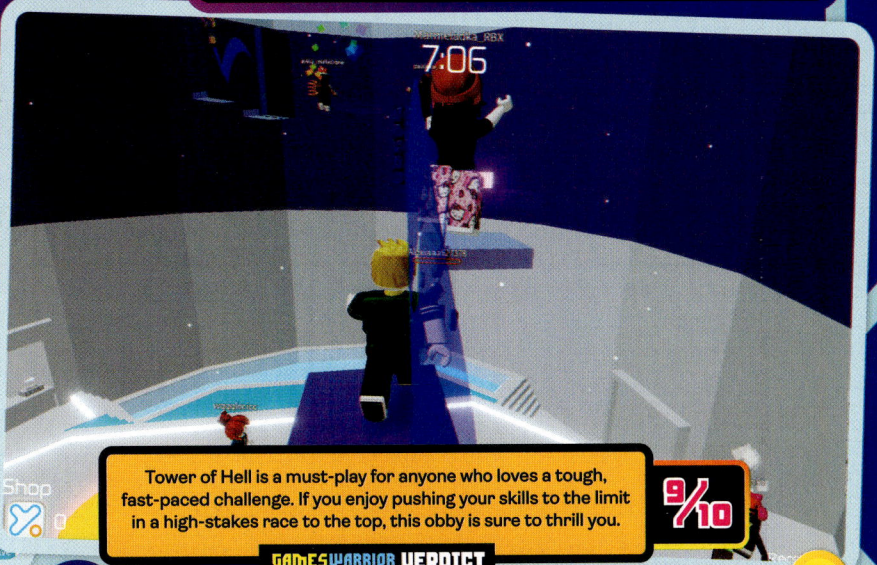

Tower of Hell is a must-play for anyone who loves a tough, fast-paced challenge. If you enjoy pushing your skills to the limit in a high-stakes race to the top, this obby is sure to thrill you.

GAMESWARRIOR VERDICT

9/10

COTTON OBBY

Cotton Obby brings a soft, whimsical twist to obstacle challenges. In this game, you navigate through a course with cotton-candy inspired visuals and gentle, bouncy obstacles that make every step feel light and fun.

WHY WE LOVE IT

- Its unique, fluffy design creates a delightful and inviting atmosphere.

- The obstacles are playful and offer a change of pace from more intense courses.

- It's perfect for those who enjoy a more relaxed, colourful challenge.

LEVEL COMPLETED!
🪙 DEATHS: 3
⏱ TIME: 5:16.00
💎 30 GEMS REWARD
GET X2 GEMS
CONTINUE

GAMESWARRIOR SAYS

If you complete a course, you're rewarded with gems which you can use to buy upgrades and extras to use in the game!

Cotton Obby is a charming experience that's ideal if you're looking for an entertaining, less stressful challenge. Its imaginative design and light-hearted obstacles make it a refreshing treat in the world of obbies.

8/10

GAMESWARRIOR VERDICT

TEAMWORK PUZZLES

Teamwork Puzzles is a cooperative obby where you and your friends work together to overcome obstacles that require both physical skill and clever problem-solving. In this game, collaboration is key as you combine your efforts to solve puzzles and navigate tricky sections of the course.

WHY WE LOVE IT

- It encourages teamwork and communication in an entertaining, obstacle-filled setting.

- The mix of physical challenges and puzzles keeps every run interesting.

- Working with friends makes the experience both engaging and full of laughs.

GAMESWARRIOR SAYS

Try switching roles with your mates – sometimes a fresh perspective on a tricky section can help everyone progress!

Teamwork Puzzles is a fantastic choice if you enjoy a shared challenge. The blend of puzzles and physical obby tasks makes it a great way to bond with friends while testing your skills together.

8/10

GAMESWARRIOR VERDICT

ESCAPE SCHOOL OBBY!

Escape School Obby! is a brilliant and exciting obby that challenges you to navigate through a school filled with obstacles and puzzles, all with the goal of escaping before time runs out. You'll find yourself in a colourful school environment where every classroom and corridor holds a new challenge to overcome. From tricky jumps to clever puzzles, the game tests your agility, timing, and problem-solving skills as you search for the key to freedom.

As you progress, the levels become increasingly intricate, ensuring that every escape attempt is a fresh and exciting adventure, with imaginative extras (like outrunning the high school football team!) thrown in for good measure!

GAMESWARRIOR SAYS

Throughout the game you'll encounter checkpoints that allow you to restart from there if you die – don't forget to trigger them!

V.1 Run time 10:33:49

Escape School is a standout obby on Roblox, brilliantly combining the entertainment of a classic escape room with the excitement of an obstacle course.

9/10

GAMESWARRIOR VERDICT

TYCOON GAMES

Ever wanted to run your own theme park, restaurant or even an entire city? Well, in Roblox you can do just that – or any one of hundreds of other businesses! Tycoon games are all about growing something amazing out of absolutely nothing, building, managing and developing your own empire! Let's dive in and see why they can be so engrossing!

WHAT DO YOU DO IN TYCOON GAMES?

In tycoon games, you control your own business. You are responsible for setting prices, designing new products, buildings, or services, hiring staff and making a profit.

HOW DO TYCOON GAMES WORK?

All tycoon games start small: you begin with a small plot of land or a basic business. From there, you use in-game money to build and upgrade. You might buy machines, hire workers, or unlock cool features. The best part? The more you build, the more money you earn to make your tycoon even bigger and better.

WHY ARE TYCOON GAMES SUCH FUN?

Tycoon games are exciting because you get to watch your little idea grow into something epic. They're perfect if you like creating, planning and seeing results. Some games even let you sample your business – riding your own rollercoaster, for example. Others let you compete with friends to see who can build the coolest business, or work together on the same project.

What's more, you can always try new strategies or explore different tycoon themes – there's always something fresh to try!

MALL TYCOON

This one is all about building and managing your own shopping centre. You start by building an empty mall, then you need to fill it with stores people will find appealing to attract more people and make more money!

WHY WE LOVE IT

• This is a simpler style of tycoon game – you run over indicators on the floor and then decide what type of shop to build, for example. You still have lots of control, but it feels gentler and less involved.

• Watching your mall grow from nothing to a thriving shopping centre is a joy. You can even get advice from customers about the kind of stores they want you to add – keeping them happy is important!

• You can visit other players' malls for inspiration and ideas!

GAMESWARRIOR SAYS

Your avatar can visit the stores you build and buy products for themselves – what better way to advertise your own stores?!

GAMESWARRIOR VERDICT

A brilliant, casual take on the tycoon genre that will keep you coming back for more! Let's go shopping!

8/10

INDUSTRIALIST

This game is all about building and managing an industrial empire. You start small, gathering resources like wood and stone, and progress to constructing factories, refineries, and power plants.

WHY WE LOVE IT

• This game involves complex production chains and intricate factory layouts so there's a lot of thinking involved!

• The game encourages automation, allowing you to create intricate production lines without having to oversee every tiny detail (which would be boring!).

• There's a lot of content and its added to regularly, so the game always feels fresh and engaging!

GAMESWARRIOR SAYS

Investing more in research means you can unlock better technologies more quickly, meaning you can really expand your industrial empire quickly and unlock more efficient technology!

GAMESWARRIOR VERDICT

It can take a little while to get the hang of this one, but the deep gameplay and creative freedom make it worth the effort if you do!

7/10

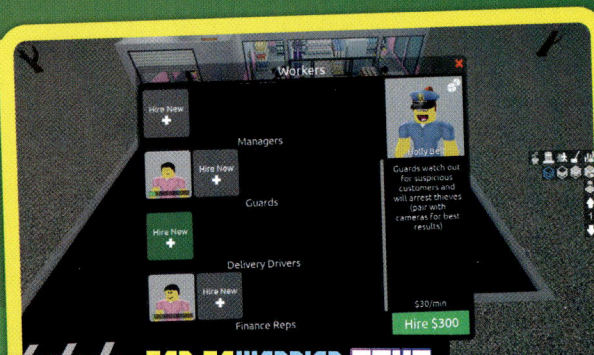

RETAIL TYCOON 2

Have you ever wanted to run your own shop? In Retail Tycoon 2, you can build and manage a store, stock products and keep customers happy.

WHY WE LOVE IT

- Begin with a small shop and choose what to sell, like toys, groceries, or electronics. As you earn money, you can expand your shop, add new items, and attract even more customers.

- There's so much fun to have by exploring the impact that adding new ranges has on how many visitors you attract!

- You can learn lots about money by seeing the difference in selling a small number of products for large profits each time, or lots of products for a small profit.

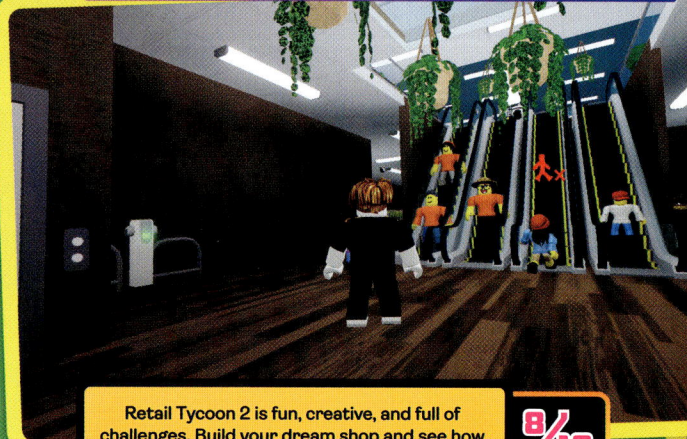

Retail Tycoon 2 is fun, creative, and full of challenges. Build your dream shop and see how far you can grow your business!

8/10

GAMESWARRIOR VERDICT

THEME PARK TYCOON 2

If you've ever dreamed of running your own theme park, Theme Park Tycoon 2 on Roblox is the game for you! It's creative, entertaining and lets you build a park full of thrilling rides and happy guests.

WHY WE LOVE IT

- Choose from exciting rides like roller coasters, ferris wheels and log flumes. You can even create custom roller coasters with loops and twists to wow your visitors!

- To keep visitors smiling, you can add food stalls, bathrooms, and seating. You can even decorate your park with trees, fountains and paths to make it more inviting.

- As your park becomes popular, you'll earn money to unlock bigger and better attractions. You can even buy more land for an even bigger park!

With so much to design and explore, we think Theme Park Tycoon 2 is a fun-filled adventure you won't want to miss. Dive in and start building today!

9/10

GAMESWARRIOR VERDICT

RESTAURANT TYCOON 2

Have you ever dreamed of running your own restaurant? In Restaurant Tycoon 2 on Roblox, you can design, build, and manage your very own eatery. It's exciting, creative, and packed with surprises!

Start by choosing a restaurant style – from cosy cafés to stylish sushi bars. With loads of decoration options, you can create a unique space that reflects your taste and personality. One of the most exciting parts of the game is the menu. You can serve food from all over the world, like burgers, sushi, and tacos. Unlocking new recipes as you progress keeps your customers happy and coming back for more.

As your restaurant grows, you can expand, upgrade your kitchen, or even open a drive-thru. We found challenges like improving customer ratings and completing tasks make the game even more exciting.

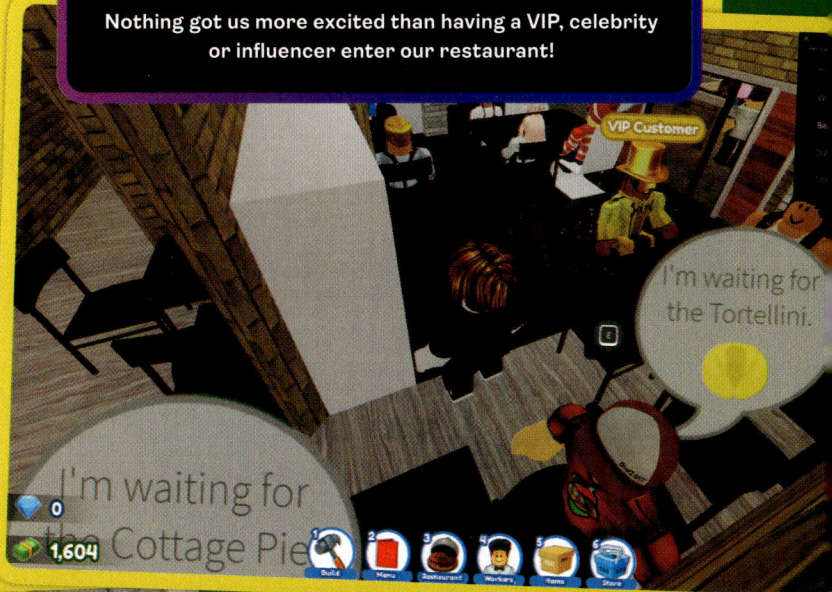

Congratulations!
You've unlocked:

Roast Dinner

Food Origins
United Kingdom

Continue

ANIMAL GAMES

Roblox is brimming with games that celebrate our love for all things animal! Whether you're keen on adopting adorable pets, managing a buzzing bee colony, galloping through open fields on horseback, or living out the life of a fierce feline warrior; there's an animal-themed game for every taste. With popular titles such as Adopt Me!, Pet Simulator, Bee Swarm Simulator, Horse Valley and Warrior Cats, these games offer a delightful blend of creativity, interaction and fun. Let's delve into the wonderful world of Roblox games featuring animals!

WHAT DO YOU DO IN ANIMAL-THEMED GAMES?

Animal-themed games on Roblox aren't just about collecting creatures — they offer a whole world of experiences where animals take centre stage in unexpected ways. You might find yourself solving mysteries as a clever fox, designing the perfect habitat in a wildlife tycoon, or competing in agility courses as a speedy dog. Some games even let you step into the wild, facing survival challenges where you must hunt, forage and avoid predators just like real animals.

HOW DO ANIMAL-THEMED GAMES WORK?

Animal-themed games on Roblox cover a broad spectrum of experiences. Some, like Adopt Me!, focus on nurturing and caring for pets within a cosy virtual home. Others, such as Pet Simulator, task you with collecting and upgrading a variety of animals to help you gather coins and treasures. Bee Swarm Simulator challenges you to manage your very own hive, gathering pollen and creating honey. In Horse Valley, you're invited to enjoy the freedom of riding and caring for horses amidst scenic surroundings, while Warrior Cats draws inspiration from the popular book series to immerse you in a world where you live as a wild feline among clans.

WHY ARE ANIMAL-THEMED GAMES SO FUN?

The charm of animal-themed games lies in the joy of interacting with cute, well-designed creatures and the satisfaction of nurturing them. These games combine imaginative worlds with social elements, allowing you to share your experiences with friends, trade animals, and take on exciting challenges together. The blend of creativity, community and the sheer delight of the animal kingdom makes these games a treasured part of the Roblox experience.

WARRIOR CATS

Warrior Cats is a role-playing game on Roblox that draws its inspiration from the beloved book series. In this immersive experience, you step into the role of a feline warrior, creating your own unique character and joining a clan to live out your own story. The game focuses on community interaction and imaginative role-play, allowing you to experience the life of a wild cat in a world that mirrors the spirit of the original novels.

WHY WE LOVE IT

- It captures the essence of the Warrior Cats series, offering an experience that feels both familiar and fresh.

- You have the chance to craft your own feline character and become part of a vibrant clan community.

- There are lots of different ways to play and things to do – hunt, forage, fight, or even just hang around homes and be a pet!

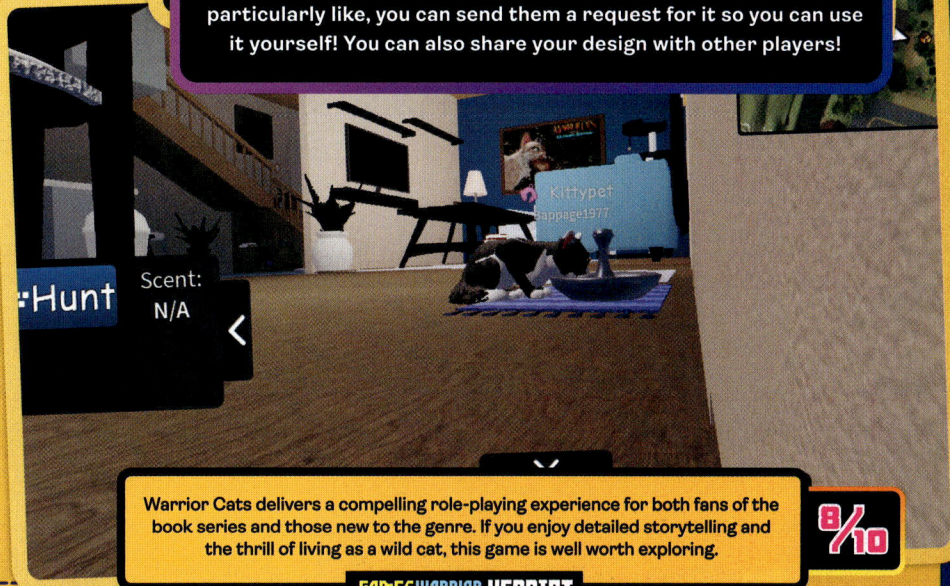

Character Exchange
Request or Send your current character design to other players here!

Anna_s033	Send / Request
Anna_s92	Send / Request
Ciasteczko_19922015	Send / Request

GAMESWARRIOR SAYS

If you spot another player with a design for their cat that you particularly like, you can send them a request for it so you can use it yourself! You can also share your design with other players!

Scent: N/A

+Hunt

Kittypet
tappage1977

Warrior Cats delivers a compelling role-playing experience for both fans of the book series and those new to the genre. If you enjoy detailed storytelling and the thrill of living as a wild cat, this game is well worth exploring.

GAMESWARRIOR VERDICT

8/10

HORSE VALLEY

Horse Valley gives you the chance to enjoy the freedom of the equine world. In this immersive experience, you can ride and care for horses while exploring a beautifully crafted landscape. The game focuses on bonding with your horse as you traverse open fields and serene vistas. It's a great way to relax!

WHY WE LOVE IT

- It offers an authentic horse riding and caring experience in a tranquil setting.

- The scenic environments provide a perfect backdrop for both relaxed exploration and exciting rides.

- Its simplicity and focus on equine interaction make every session both refreshing and memorable.

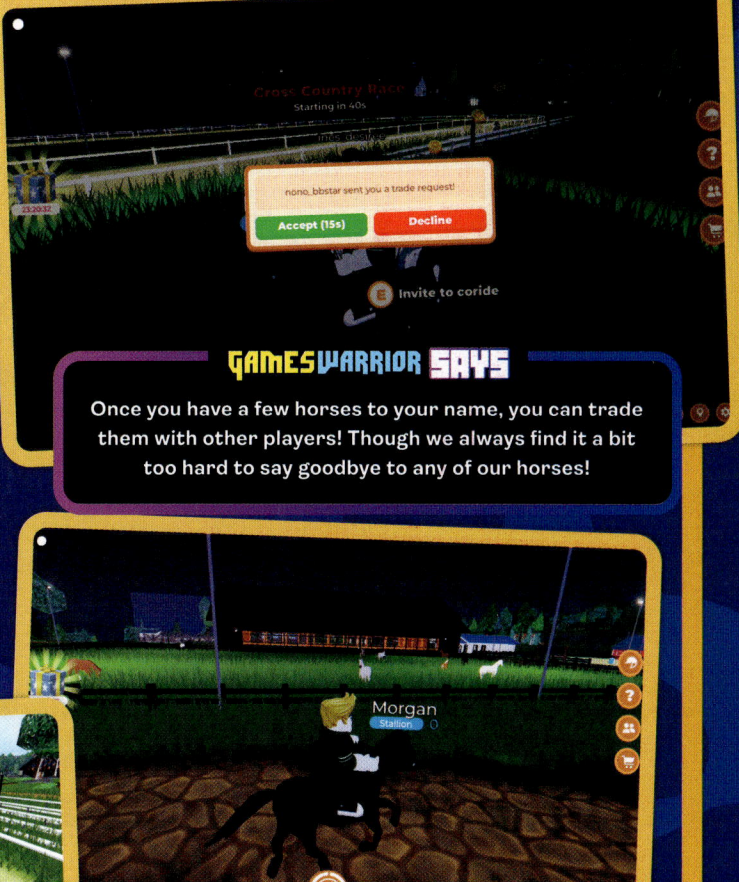

Cross Country Race
Starting in 40s

nono, bbstar sent you a trade request!
Accept (15s)   Decline

Invite to coride

GAMESWARRIOR SAYS

Once you have a few horses to your name, you can trade them with other players! Though we always find it a bit too hard to say goodbye to any of our horses!

Morgan
Stallion

Charming and calming, Horse Valley provides a delightful escape into the world of equine adventures. With its inviting landscapes and interesting gameplay, it is a must-try for any horse enthusiast.

GAMESWARRIOR VERDICT

8/10

BEE SWARM SIMULATOR

Bee Swarm Simulator invites you to take on the role of a beekeeper, venturing into vibrant fields to gather pollen which you then convert into honey. As you explore the colourful world, you have the opportunity to upgrade your bees and equipment, adding a layer of strategy to the playful adventure. Like all great games, the idea is simple, but the more you play, the more layers to the gameplay are revealed and the more you want to keep playing!

GAMESWARRIOR SAYS

Feeding treats to your bees can help them to level up, making them more productive workers in the process!

WHY WE LOVE IT

- The game offers a delightful blend of beekeeping and exploration, making each session both fun and rewarding.

- Its engaging mechanics allow you to see real progress as you grow your colony and earn various rewards.

- A friendly community and regular updates ensure that the experience remains fresh and exciting.

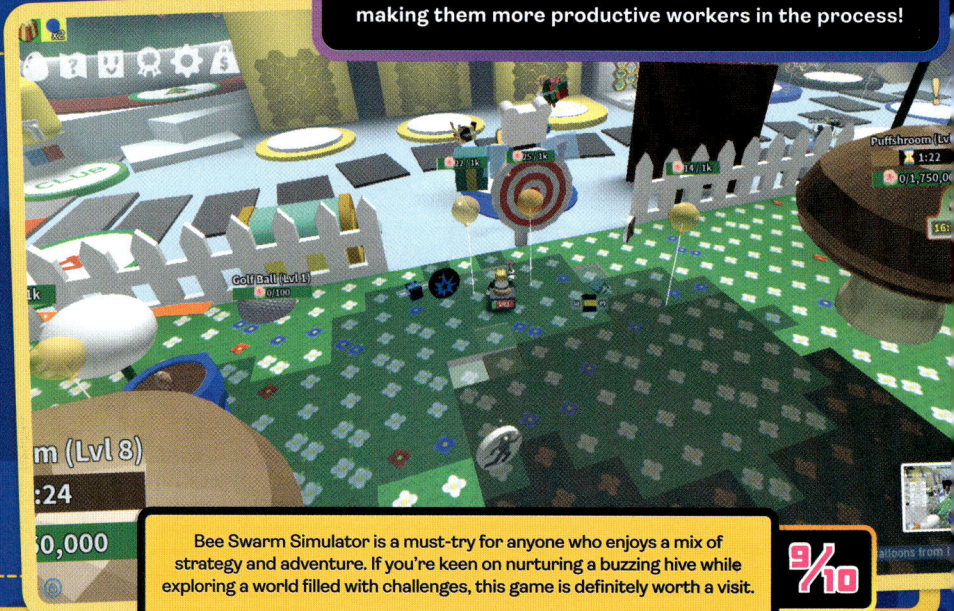

Bee Swarm Simulator is a must-try for anyone who enjoys a mix of strategy and adventure. If you're keen on nurturing a buzzing hive while exploring a world filled with challenges, this game is definitely worth a visit.

9/10

GAMESWARRIOR VERDICT

PET SIMULATOR 99!

Pet Simulator 99! sees you collecting and nurturing a variety of pets while gathering coins to pay for it all. As you navigate through the maps, your pets help you pick up rewards, making every adventure an opportunity to expand your pet collection and enhance your abilities. The focus is on the thrill of exploration and the satisfaction of uncovering rare finds, ensuring that each session is as rewarding as it is fun.

WHY WE LOVE IT

- The seamless blend of exploration and collection creates a truly engaging experience.

- Upgrading your pets adds a satisfying layer of progression to the gameplay.

- With over 200 zones and a lively community around the game, life in Pet Simulator 99! is NEVER quiet!

GAMESWARRIOR SAYS

As you progress you can use in-game currency to equip more and more pets at once – which in turn helps you gain more money!

Pet Simulator 99! is ideal if you like the gentle nature of slowly building and nurturing your pet over time!

9/10

GAMESWARRIOR VERDICT

ADOPT ME!

Adopt Me! has become one of Roblox's most celebrated social experiences, a vibrant world where the joy of pet adoption meets imaginative role-play. You begin your adventure by exploring a bustling neighbourhood filled with opportunities to adopt a variety of pets, each offering its own charm and personality. Caring for your pet and customising your home creates a warm, engaging atmosphere that draws you in, making every session feel like a new chapter in your virtual life.

The game's design encourages creative expression and social interaction, with features that allow you to trade pets, decorate your living space, and join community events. Regular updates and seasonal events ensure there is always fresh content to discover, keeping the experience both dynamic and exciting. Whether you're building your dream home, nurturing your pet, or simply enjoying the lively interactions with other players, Adopt Me! offers endless possibilities for imaginative play and personal expression.

GAMESWARRIOR SAYS

We love how you can just stroke and play with your pet to fill him or her with happiness whenever you feel like it!

GAMESWARRIOR VERDICT

Adopt Me! stands as a landmark title on Roblox, blending the charm of pet care with the excitement of community-driven role-play. It is a must-play for anyone who enjoys creativity, social interaction and the delightful surprises that come with exploring a lively virtual world.

10/10

SIMULATION GAMES

Roblox is home to countless creative experiences and simulation games are one of its most popular categories. These games invite you to step into different roles – like running a business or providing a service – so you can get a taste of real-world tasks in a light-hearted, interactive way. Whether you're flipping pizzas, helping hospital patients, or even responding to emergencies, there's a simulation game to spark your imagination.

HOW DO SIMULATION GAMES WORK?

Simulation games in Roblox recreate everyday jobs or situations. You'll usually have tasks or responsibilities – like cooking, cleaning, or managing money – to keep your virtual business or role running smoothly. Most games reward you with in-game cash or items for completing tasks successfully.

WHY ARE SIMULATION GAMES SO FUN?

Simulation games are a brilliant way to experience different jobs without any real-world stress. They blend creativity, teamwork, and problem-solving, making every shift or task feel fresh and exciting. Plus, playing with friends or other Roblox users adds a social element that keeps you coming back for more!

WHAT DO YOU DO IN SIMULATION GAMES?

Depending on the game, you might take on roles such as a cashier, chef, hotel manager, or even a firefighter. You'll interact with other players, earn money or points and use them to improve your workspace, home, or equipment. It's all about stepping into a new job, learning the ropes and having fun while doing it.

WELCOME TO BLOXBURG

Welcome to Bloxburg is a hugely popular life-simulation game where you can build and decorate your dream home, get a job, and live out a virtual day-to-day routine. You earn money by working at various businesses around town – like delivering pizzas or stocking shelves – then spend your earnings on everything from furniture to vehicles.

GAMESWARRIOR SAYS

Although you can chop and change jobs to make things interesting, if you stick at one job and get steadily better at it, your earning potential will rise so you can make more money quickly!

WHY WE LOVE IT

- Lets you design your own house, from cosy cottages to grand mansions.

- Multiple job options keep the gameplay fresh and rewarding.

- Offers a relaxed, open-world environment for endless roleplay fun.

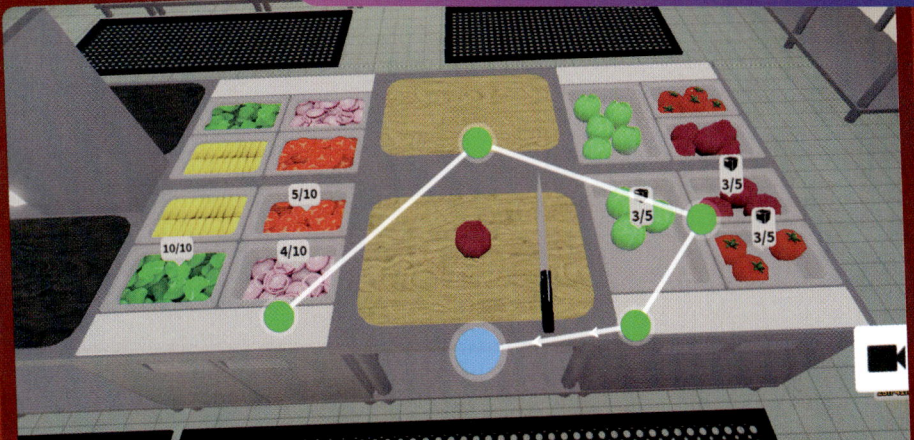

If you enjoy building, customising and exploring at your own pace, Welcome to Bloxburg is an absolute treat. With a huge community and constant updates, it's perfect for creative souls.

GAMESWARRIOR VERDICT 9/10

WORK AT A HOTEL!

If you've ever wondered what it's like to run a hotel, Work at a Hotel! is the perfect simulation game for you! Whether you're checking in guests, cleaning rooms, or even managing the front desk, there's always something to do. Plus, you can climb the ranks to unlock even more exciting responsibilities.

GAMESWARRIOR SAYS

Make friends with co-workers! Teamwork makes running the hotel much smoother.

WHY WE LOVE IT

- You can take on different hotel roles, from receptionist to manager.

- The hotel is always busy with guests, making every shift interesting.

- Working with other players makes it an enjoyable, team-based experience.

Work at a Hotel! is a great game for anyone who loves roleplaying and working as a team. It's challenging, exciting, and a great way to experience life in the hospitality industry – Roblox style!

GAMESWARRIOR VERDICT 8/10

MAPLE HOSPITAL

Maple Hospital puts you in the heart of the medical world, allowing you to roleplay as doctors, nurses, patients and more. From diagnosing illnesses to performing surgeries, every aspect of hospital life is covered in a friendly, interactive setting.

WHY WE LOVE IT

- Realistic hospital equipment and detailed wards add to the immersion.

- Multiple roles keep the gameplay varied and exciting.

- Cooperative play fosters teamwork and communication.

GAMESWARRIOR SAYS

Keep an eye on patient chat – sometimes they'll drop hints about their symptoms, making it easier to diagnose them quickly!

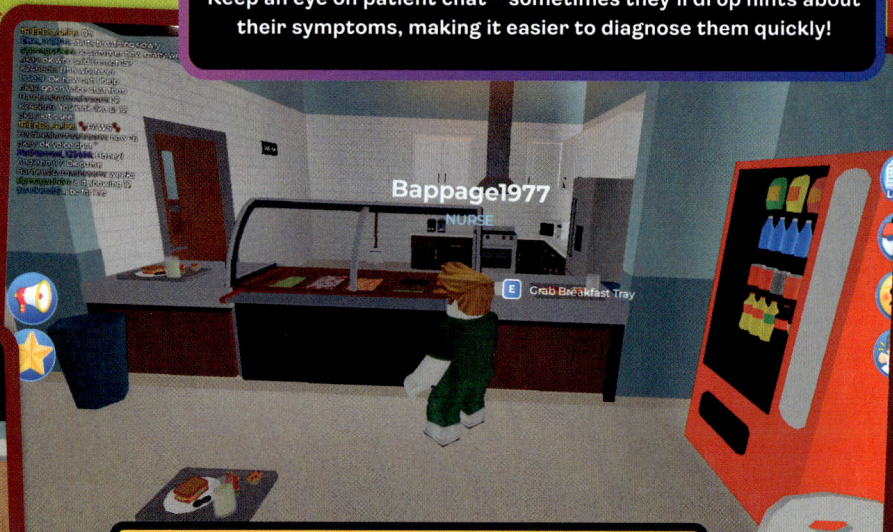

If you love helping others and discovering what it's like to work in healthcare, Maple Hospital is a brilliant and detailed simulation. It's also a great way to learn a bit about how hospitals operate.

9/10

GAMESWARRIOR VERDICT

WORK AT A PIZZA PLACE

Work at a Pizza Place is a Roblox classic that's been delighting players for years. You can take orders, cook pizzas, box them up, and deliver them to hungry customers – earning money to spend on your in-game house.

WHY WE LOVE IT

- Frantic, fast-paced gameplay with lots of roles to try.

- Cooperative tasks mean you'll need to work as a team to keep the pizza shop running.

- You can customise your house and show off your decorating skills.

GAMESWARRIOR SAYS

You can take on every role in a pizza place you can think of – cashier, cook, delivery driver and even supplier! Each job has different challenges to keep you playing for longer!

With its mix of cooking, delivery, and teamwork, Work at a Pizza Place remains one of the most engaging simulation games on Roblox. It's perfect for players who love multitasking and a lively atmosphere.

10/10

GAMESWARRIOR VERDICT

Citizens: 2

FIREFIGHTERS!

Ever dreamed of being a real firefighter? In Firefighters!, you'll step into the boots of a brave emergency worker, responding to fires, crashes, and rescues across a realistic city. This game is packed with fire engines, firefighting tools, and challenging missions that make every call exciting.

One of the best parts of Firefighters! is how teamwork-focused it is. You and your crew must coordinate your response, making sure fires are put out and civilians are rescued safely. The game even includes different fire stations, working sirens and a variety of rescue vehicles, making it one of the most realistic emergency services games on Roblox.

The missions vary from small house fires to huge building blazes, keeping the action unpredictable and engaging. You'll need to master firefighting techniques, from using hoses to breaking down doors, and even operating heavy rescue equipment. The better you do, the more you can upgrade your gear and unlock new roles, making every shift more exciting.

If you love simulation games that feel realistic and require teamwork, Firefighters! is an absolute must-play. Grab your gear, slide down the fire station pole, and get ready to save the day!

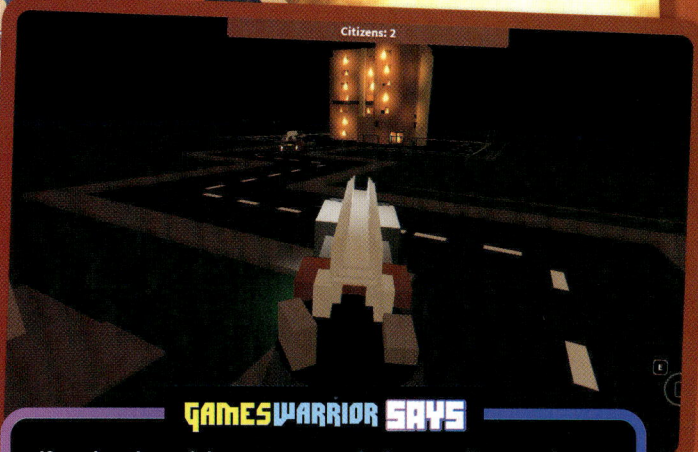

GAMESWARRIOR SAYS

If you're the quickest to respond when a call comes in and get to the fire engine first, you can drive it to the fire!

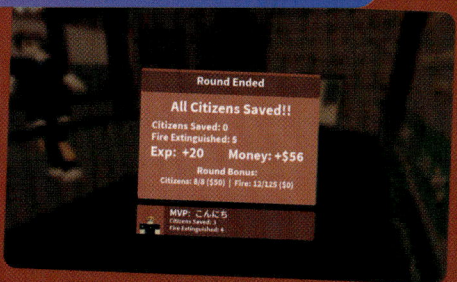

Firefighters! is one of the most thrilling simulation games in Roblox. If you love action-packed, team-based challenges, this game will keep you on the edge of your seat!

GAMESWARRIOR VERDICT

10/10

DRIVING GAMES

Roblox is home to some of the most thrilling driving experiences you can imagine! Whether you want to race at high speeds, explore vast open roads, or customise the ultimate dream car, there's a driving game for every petrolhead. Let's buckle up and take a look at the exciting world of Roblox driving games!

WHAT DO YOU DO IN DRIVING GAMES?

You'll be burning rubber, mastering sharp turns, and competing against others to prove you're the fastest on the road. Some games focus on head-to-head races, demanding quick reflexes and strategic cornering, while others encourage exploration, letting you drive across stunning landscapes. Many offer deep customisation, allowing you to fine-tune your car's performance, paint job, and even add special modifications.

WHY ARE DRIVING GAMES SO FUN?

There's nothing quite like the rush of speed, the thrill of overtaking an opponent on the final lap, or the satisfaction of pulling off the perfect drift. Roblox driving games bring these experiences to life in unique and creative ways, with exciting challenges, realistic physics, and incredible car designs. The ability to race against friends, explore massive worlds, or build your ultimate dream car makes driving games some of the most exhilarating experiences on Roblox!

HOW DO DRIVING GAMES WORK?

Driving games on Roblox come in many forms. Some focus on high-speed racing, where precision and skill determine the winner; while others offer expansive open worlds where you can cruise freely and explore. Some games let you take on the role of a professional driver, drifting through tight corners, while others are all about building and customising your vehicle. Many feature progression systems, allowing you to earn in-game currency to buy better cars, unlock new tracks, or upgrade your driving abilities.

MOTO TRACKDAY PROJECT

If you like your racing of the two-wheeled variety then look no further than Moto Trackday Project, a racing extravaganza that combines street racing with track racing! Upgrade your bike, buy new helmets and try to establish yourself as the fastest thing on two wheels!

WHY WE LOVE IT

- The physics in the game are really good – if you accelerate too hard then you'll end up doing a wheelie, and you'll need to really slow down for corners!

- There are plenty of street circuit races to take on, so by the time you can afford a race bike, you'll be ready for the challenge!

- It's a lively online community with lots of chat, and regular updates to the game – including new tracks!

GAMESWARRIOR SAYS

You can take part in various street races to build up your finances – and you get a cheeky little bonus if you finish first too!

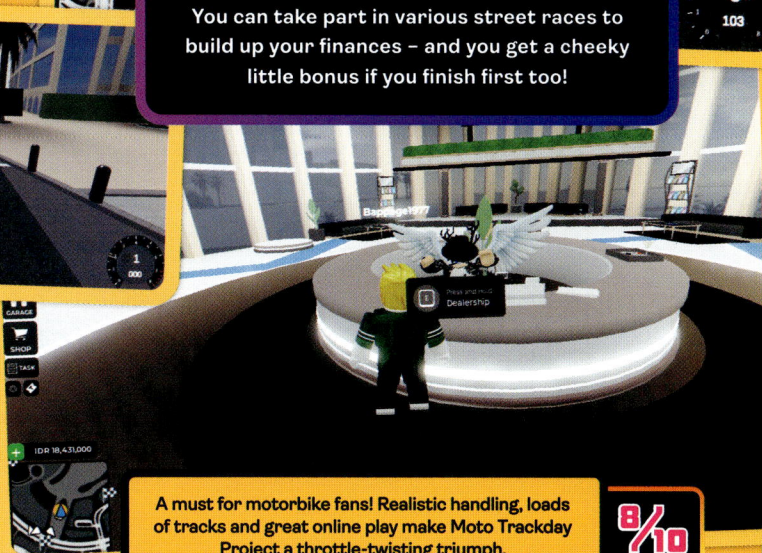

A must for motorbike fans! Realistic handling, loads of tracks and great online play make Moto Trackday Project a throttle-twisting triumph.

GAMESWARRIOR VERDICT

8/10

TAXI BOSS

This is one of the most immersive games we've ever played in the Roblox universe! As a taxi driver, you must head around the city picking people up and taking them to their destinations – but it merges tycoon game elements as you build your own taxi company in the process!

WHY WE LOVE IT

- It's a busy city with different districts so you'll soon learn where you can pick up good fares and where to avoid.

- Hiring extra drivers brings in a solid stream of money even when you're not out driving yourself!

- As you earn more money, you can buy better cars to use, attracting a higher class of customer.

GAMESWARRIOR SAYS

When you set up your office, you even get to decide on your corporate logo, as well as hiring drivers and mechanics to keep the business running smoothly.

Brilliantly combining a driving game with extra tycoon elements, Taxi Boss will swallow hours and hours of your life if you aren't careful!

GAMESWARRIOR VERDICT

9/10

BRITISH RAILWAY

Time for a change of pace when it comes to driving fun. British Railway puts you in charge of driving a variety of real trains between real British train stations. It sounds like it would be a snooze fest but in fact, it's brilliant fun.

WHY WE LOVE IT

- A well put-together tutorial means that you will be able to get to grips with everything quickly.

- Keeping to schedule and picking up passengers earns you money – the closer you are to schedule, the more passengers you get!

- It's not as simple as starting and stopping! There are schedules to stick to, speed limits to observe and stop signals that must be obeyed!

The most exciting piece of dullness you'll ever play.

GAMESWARRIOR VERDICT

9/10

ROBLOX RALLY RACING

When it comes to exciting driving experiences, it's hard to find anything more varied and challenging than rally racing. This awesome game faithfully brings rally racing into the Roblox universe – you'll quickly find yourself throwing high-powered cars down tiny country lanes, taking blind turns with only your co-driver's shouted instructions to help you!

WHY WE LOVE IT

- There's so much choice! The game features over 45 different cars and almost 20 tracks to race on so it never feels the same twice!

- The sound is particularly great, capturing that distinctive rally feel, and the handling is also great – as you'll know once you start powersliding round those bends!

- To help, you get your own co-driver who will give handy directions – which also pop up on screen – about upcoming turns and obstacles!

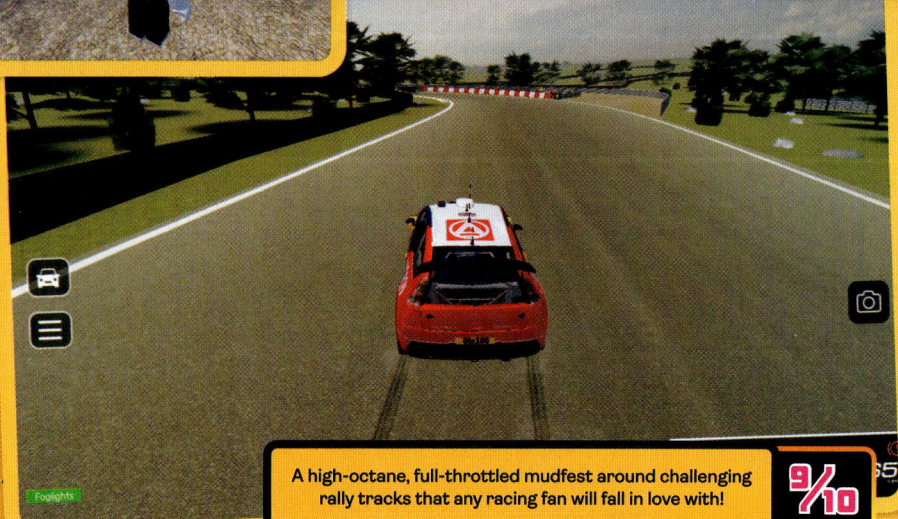

A high-octane, full-throttled mudfest around challenging rally tracks that any racing fan will fall in love with!

GAMESWARRIOR VERDICT

9/10

FORMULA APEX RACING

AAAAAND THERE GOES ROBLOX LEGEND RACER!
If you're an F1 petrolhead then this is absolutely the game for you. Formula Apex Racing is all about the world's leading motorsport brand, and it offers an incredibly lifelike experience.

The game features ten real-word tracks with four more designed by the developers. More tracks are added often too, as part of a very vibrant community. As well as the tracks, the cars are super realistic too, and you can select cars from different F1 eras.

To add to the fun you can decorate the liveries (car paint jobs!) and choose helmets from F1 legends of the past. You'll earn the money to do this as you race, so the more you put in, the more you'll get out of it!

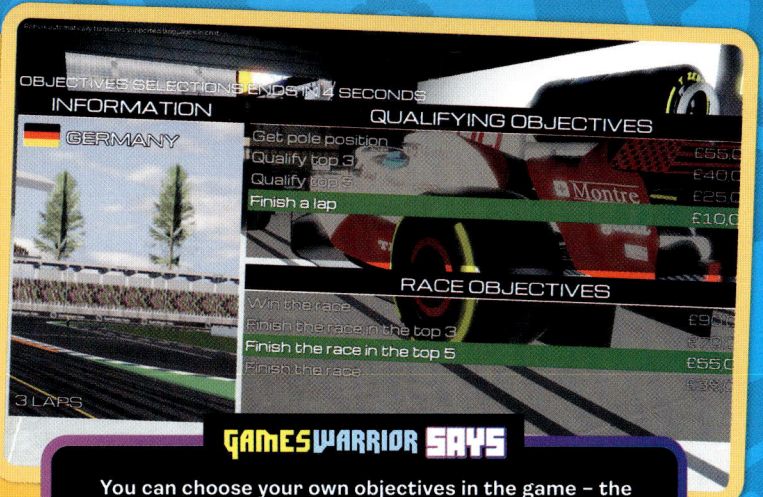

GAMESWARRIOR SAYS

You can choose your own objectives in the game – the lower your target, the less money you get for achieving it. Dare you back yourself to be a race winner?

GAMESWARRIOR VERDICT

An incredible achievement that is head and shoulders above any other racing experience in Roblox. If you like racers, you HAVE to play this!

10/10

BUILDING GAMES

Roblox is celebrated for its creative potential, and building games are a shining example of what the game is all about. These games invite you to craft innovative structures and tackle unique challenges. Whether you're building a sturdy raft to brave water obstacles, designing an aircraft that defies gravity, or transforming a blank island into a personalised masterpiece, these games are perfect examples of the creative gameplay that makes Roblox so brilliant!

WHAT DO YOU DO IN BUILDING GAMES?

In these games, you dive straight into creative challenges that require you to design, build and innovate. You might be creating a raft to navigate tricky water passages, engineering a plane to take flight, or designing an entire island from scratch. Each game offers its own set of tasks, encouraging you to experiment with design techniques, resource management and problem-solving skills.

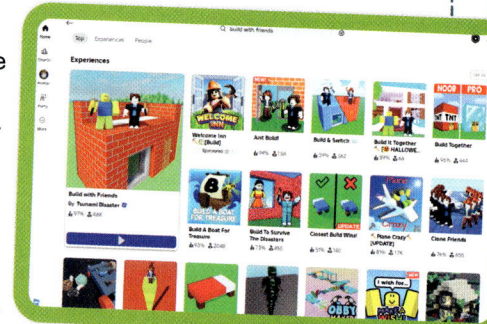

HOW DO BUILDING GAMES WORK?

Building games challenge you to shape your environment to meet specific objectives. You're usually provided with an array of materials and tools, which you use to design structures that not only work, but look great too! Whether it's a timed challenge or a collaborative project, these games test your ability to balance creativity with practicality.

WHY ARE BUILDING GAMES SO FUN?

The thrill of building games lies in the freedom they offer – the ability to transform simple blocks into functional creations or stunning works of art. They give you the chance to learn, experiment, and showcase your ingenuity. Whether you're competing solo or collaborating with friends, building games on Roblox are a celebration of creativity.

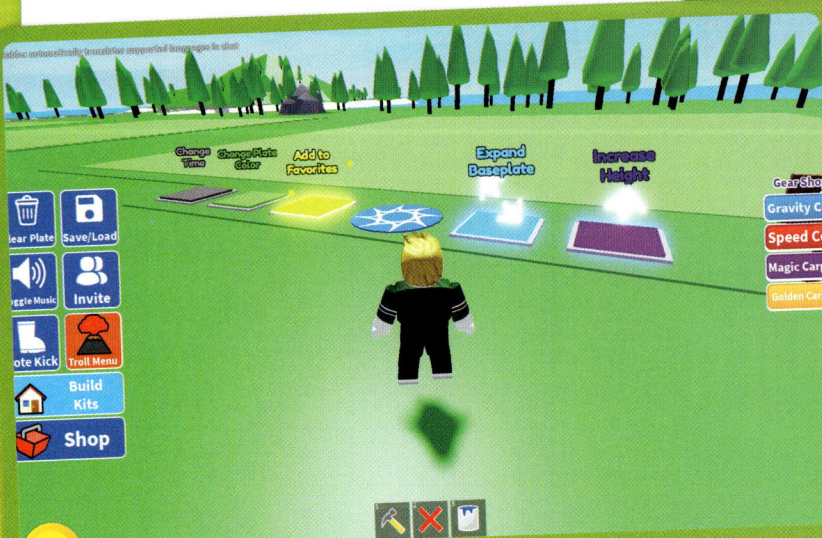

BUILD A RAFT OR DIE

Build a Raft or Die does pretty much what you'd expect – challenges you to construct a raft that can survive ever-increasingly difficult water obstacles. It will see you putting your creativity and resource management skills to the test.

GAMESWARRIOR SAYS

Experiment with different raft materials – tougher materials can help you get further!

WHY WE LOVE IT

- It challenges you to balance design aesthetics with practical functionality.

- The game encourages quick thinking and efficient use of available resources.

- Its focus on practical building provides a refreshing twist on creative challenges.

Build a Raft or Die is a must-try for anyone keen to apply their building skills in a practical setting. Its emphasis on functionality and inventive problem-solving makes it a standout experience among Roblox building games.

8/10

GAMESWARRIOR VERDICT

PLANE CRAZY

Plane Crazy invites you to channel your inner aeronautical engineer within Roblox's creative space. In this challenge, you design and construct your own aircraft, testing your ingenuity and engineering skills with every build.

WHY WE LOVE IT

- It stimulates creativity by blending design with basic principles of aerodynamics.

- The challenge pushes you to think innovatively and experiment with unconventional designs.

- It offers a unique twist on building games by combining construction with the concept of flight.

GAMESWARRIOR SAYS

Don't be afraid to try unexpected designs – sometimes an unconventional approach can yield an aircraft that surprises you with its effectiveness!

Plane Crazy is an engaging test of your creative and engineering abilities. If you're excited by the idea of exploring the possibilities of Roblox's building tools with a focus on flight, this game is well worth a try.

8/10

GAMESWARRIOR VERDICT

BUILD TO SURVIVE!

In this game, you must use your building skills to keep safe from oncoming threats. The disasters keep on coming, so you must quickly construct shelters and fortifications to outlast waves of obstacles. Every round pushes you to think on your feet, making sure your creations are both sturdy and smart.

WHY WE LOVE IT

- It challenges you to build quickly under pressure.

- The mix of survival and creativity keeps each round exciting.

- Every playthrough offers a new layout and challenge.

JUST BUILD!

Just Build! is a fantastic sandbox game that lets you unleash your creativity without any strict challenges. In this open-ended experience, you can design and construct anything you imagine, from towering castles to futuristic cities. It's all about exploring your creative side and enjoying the art of building at your own pace.

WHY WE LOVE IT

- It gives you unlimited creative freedom.

- The intuitive building tools make designing quick and easy.

- It's a relaxing escape where your imagination is the only limit.

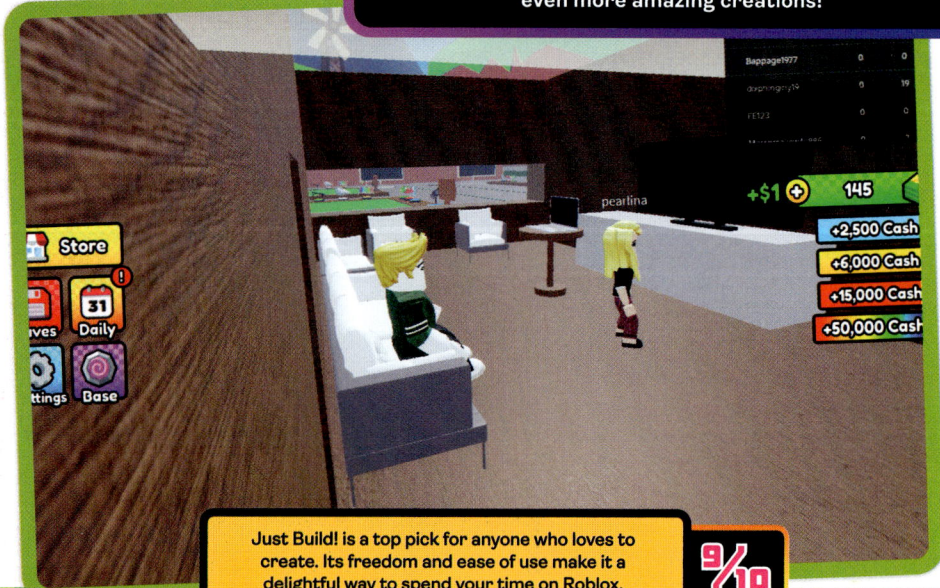

BUILD WITH FRIENDS

Build with Friends is a standout Roblox game that brings the magic of teamwork and creativity together. In this collaborative experience, you join up with your mates to design and construct impressive structures while tackling building challenges as a team. The game's focus on cooperation means that every project is a shared adventure, where planning and communication are just as important as the building itself.

In Build with Friends, you have access to a variety of versatile tools that let you craft everything from cosy homes to towering skyscrapers. The game encourages you to work together, pooling your ideas and skills to create designs that you might not have thought of on your own. It's not just about building – it's about learning from each other, having fun and celebrating your collective creativity.

The vibrant atmosphere of Build with Friends makes every session feel like a creative festival. The game regularly hosts challenges and competitions that add an extra layer of excitement, pushing you and your team to experiment with new design techniques. Whether you're planning a complex project or simply enjoying the process of creation, this game offers endless opportunities to grow and showcase your building talents.

Disaster Troll Menu

Nuke Map — Spawns a explosion above the map! 299

Tsunami — Spawns a Tsunami that will flood the map! 99

Lava Wave — Spawns a Lava Wave that floods the map with lava! 149

Zombie Invasion — Spawns a bunch of zombies that will chase you around! 49

GAMESWARRIOR SAYS

You can buy disasters to wreak havoc on your map if you want to see how your house would survive!

Build with Friends is a brilliant example of what can happen when creativity meets collaboration on Roblox. For anyone who enjoys building with mates and tackling creative challenges together, this game is an absolute must-play.

10/10

GAMESWARRIOR VERDICT

SCARY GAMES

Roblox isn't just about fun and creativity – it also offers a spookier side with its scary games. These games let you step into eerie worlds filled with creepy characters and mysterious challenges that will give you a little shiver down your spine. Whether it's escaping from a terrifying creature or solving a spooky mystery, scary games are a brilliant way to experience thrills in a safe, virtual environment. So if you're ready for a bit of spooky entertainment, read on and discover some of the most exciting scary games on Roblox!

WHAT DO YOU DO IN SCARY GAMES?

In these games, you might need to escape from a scary character, solve puzzles to uncover hidden secrets, or explore creepy locations. Sometimes you work alone, while other times you join your friends to solve mysteries together. The aim is to overcome your fears and enjoy the thrill of the unknown.

HOW DO SCARY GAMES WORK?

Scary games in Roblox are designed to create a spooky atmosphere with mysterious plots and unexpected jump-scares. They often mix puzzles, chase scenes, and eerie music to set the mood, giving you a fun challenge while keeping you on your toes.

WHY ARE SCARY GAMES SO FUN?

The joy of scary games lies in the exciting mix of challenge and mystery. They let you experience a safe dose of fright and excitement, all within a colourful and creative world. And best of all, every scary adventure helps boost your bravery!

PIGGY

Piggy is a popular game that mixes a bit of horror with a fun survival challenge. In this game, you must escape from a character inspired by Peppa Pig, all while solving puzzles and avoiding traps. The game's spooky setting and clever design make it a thrilling experience without being too scary (it is Peppa Pig, after all!)

WHY WE LOVE IT

- The puzzles require clever problem-solving and spark your imagination. They constantly challenge you to work out the best way to unlock clues and advance.

- Piggy sets a slightly sinister mood with dim lighting and mysterious sounds that give you a fun chill. This balanced ambience is just right for young players who will enjoy a bit of a thrill without getting too scared.

- The chase scenes are fast-paced and full of adrenaline, making every escape feel like a mini adventure. Running through corridors and dodging obstacles adds an exciting burst of energy to each game session.

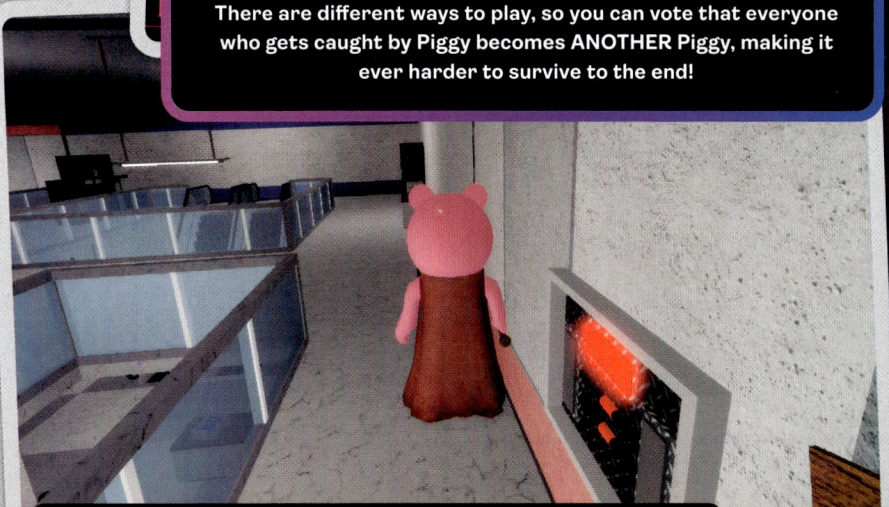

Players in Lobby

Bappage1977   pochis20788
bonnie

Piggy Voting - 6

Bot	Player	Player + Bot
0	0	0
Infection	Traitor	Swarm

GAMESWARRIOR SAYS

There are different ways to play, so you can vote that everyone who gets caught by Piggy becomes ANOTHER Piggy, making it ever harder to survive to the end!

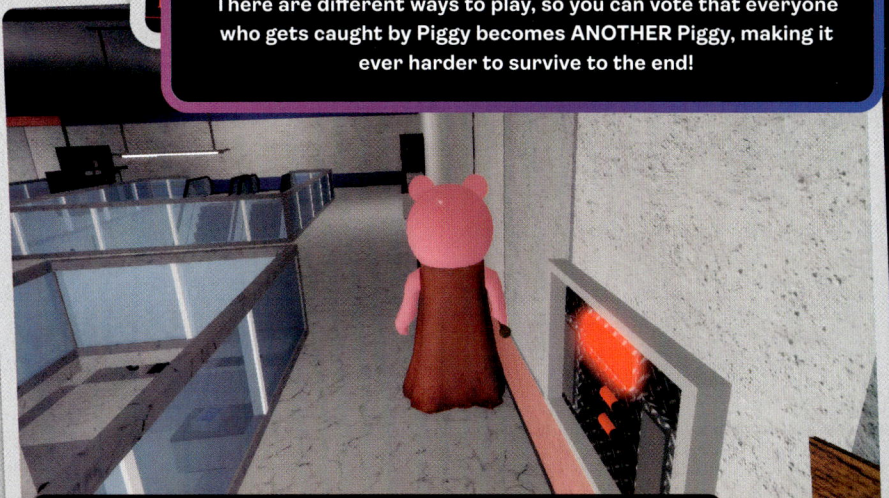

Piggy is perfect for young players who love a bit of spooky adventure. It combines mystery and action in a way that is both thrilling and safe.

9/10

GAMESWARRIOR VERDICT

BEAR (ALPHA)

Bear (Alpha) puts you in a spooky chase where a mysterious bear plushy is on the hunt. You must use your wits and quick reflexes to avoid getting caught while exploring a creepy environment. The mix of simple puzzles and exciting chase moments creates a fun, adrenaline-pumping experience.

WHY WE LOVE IT

- You never know when Bear will strike, so you must stay alert and think fast. Every round feels different, keeping the tension high and the gameplay exciting.

- The dark maps, eerie music and spooky sound effects create a chilling vibe without being too scary. It's just the right mix of creepy and fun for young players who love a thrill.

- You can work together with other players to solve puzzles and survive longer. Co-operating with friends makes each round even more enjoyable!

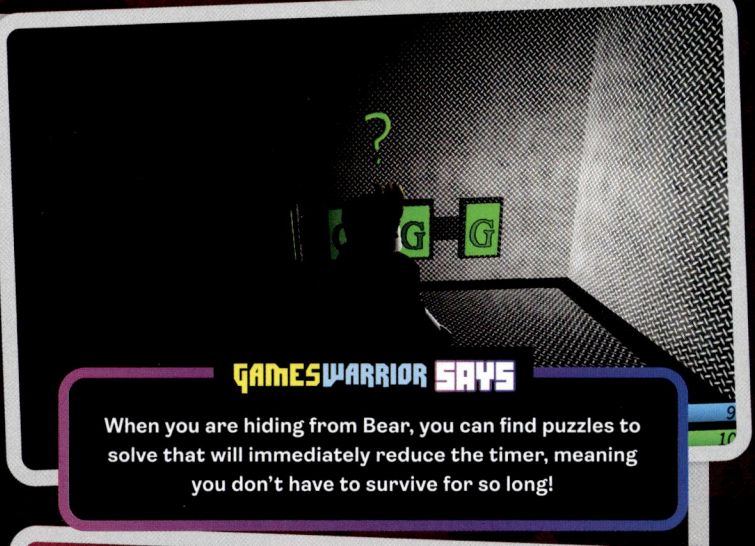

GAMESWARRIOR SAYS

When you are hiding from Bear, you can find puzzles to solve that will immediately reduce the timer, meaning you don't have to survive for so long!

If you enjoy a fun, heart-pounding chase and a spooky setting, this is a great game to try. It's scary enough to be exciting without being too frightening.

8/10

GAMESWARRIOR VERDICT

THOSE WHO REMAIN

Get ready to battle hordes of zombies in this action-packed game! It throws you into a town overrun by waves of the undead, and it's up to you to fight back! Grab your weapons, team up with friends and see how long you can survive the zombie onslaught.

WHY WE LOVE IT

- There are loads of awesome weapons to choose from, like pistols, shotguns, and even pool cues! Blast those zombies to smithereens!

- The zombies come in all shapes and sizes, so you'll need to use different tactics to defeat them. It's a real challenge!

- There are different maps to explore, each with its own unique challenges and secrets. Keep your eyes peeled for cool new areas!

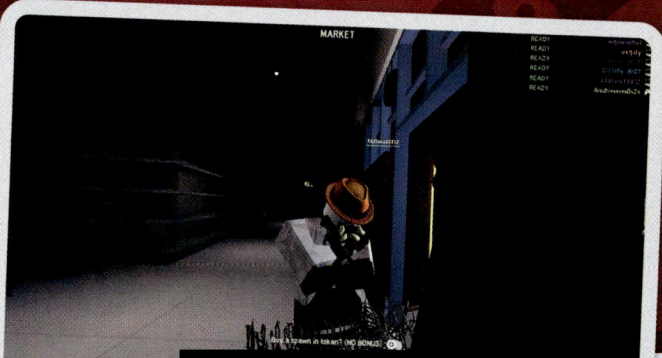

GAMESWARRIOR SAYS

You can build traps and barriers to slow down the zombie advances, giving you time to plan your counterattack!

If you like action-packed games where you get to blast zombies with awesome weapons, then this is right up your street! Just don't forget to bring your friends!

8/10

GAMESWARRIOR VERDICT

SURVIVE 100 DAYS IN HELL

Survive 100 Days in Hell is a Roblox game that dares you to brave a series of eerie challenges over a long stretch of time. You must navigate through a spooky environment and overcome various obstacles each day, testing your ability to stay calm under pressure. The game's setting is a fun blend of scary and challenging, making it a unique experience.

WHY WE LOVE IT

- You have to gather resources, fight off enemies and find ways to stay alive for 100 days. Every decision matters, making survival both challenging and rewarding.

- From swarms of zombies to other horrifying monsters, danger is always around the corner. You'll need quick reflexes and smart tactics to make it through.

- As the days go by, the enemies become stronger and the challenges get tougher. This keeps the game exciting and pushes you to improve your strategy!

GAMESWARRIOR SAYS

Just when you think endless demon attacks are your biggest worry, the lava level will begin to rise leaving you scrambling to find a safe spot!

Survive 100 Days in Hell is an exciting game for those who love a good challenge with a spooky twist! If you enjoy testing your bravery and skill in a fun, eerie environment, this game is a must-try!

8/10

GAMESWARRIOR VERDICT

Victory!

ChloeBlossom123455

MURDER MYSTERY 2

Murder Mystery 2 is one of the most popular and exciting Roblox games that brings a thrilling mystery to life. In this game, players are randomly assigned roles – some are innocents, one is the murderer and one is the sheriff. The innocents must try to stay safe and avoid the murderer, while the sheriff works to uncover clues and stop the bad guy. It's a game of wits and quick thinking, where everyone has a role to play in solving the mystery.

The game's charm lies in its mix of suspense and teamwork. As an innocent, you must watch your back and look for hints that might reveal who the murderer is. The sheriff, on the other hand, has the exciting responsibility of catching the culprit before anyone gets hurt. As for the murderer, it's all about moving stealthily and outsmarting everyone else. Every round is different, which means you never know what will happen next – a twist or a surprise is always just around the corner.

Murder Mystery 2 is designed to be exciting and engaging for players of all ages. Its cartoonish graphics and playful sound effects ensure that while the theme is spooky, the game remains friendly and accessible for young players. It's a brilliant way to practise your detective skills, work together with friends and enjoy a thrilling game of hide and seek with a twist.

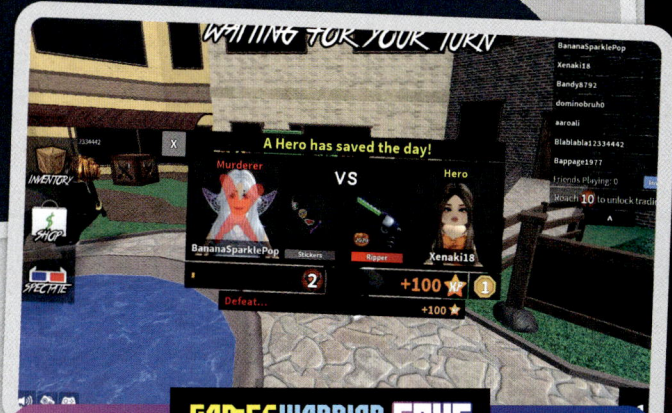

GAMESWARRIOR SAYS

It's great fun the way the game switches up your role between rounds – playing as both the sheriff and an innocent can give you a whole new perspective on the game's clever clues!

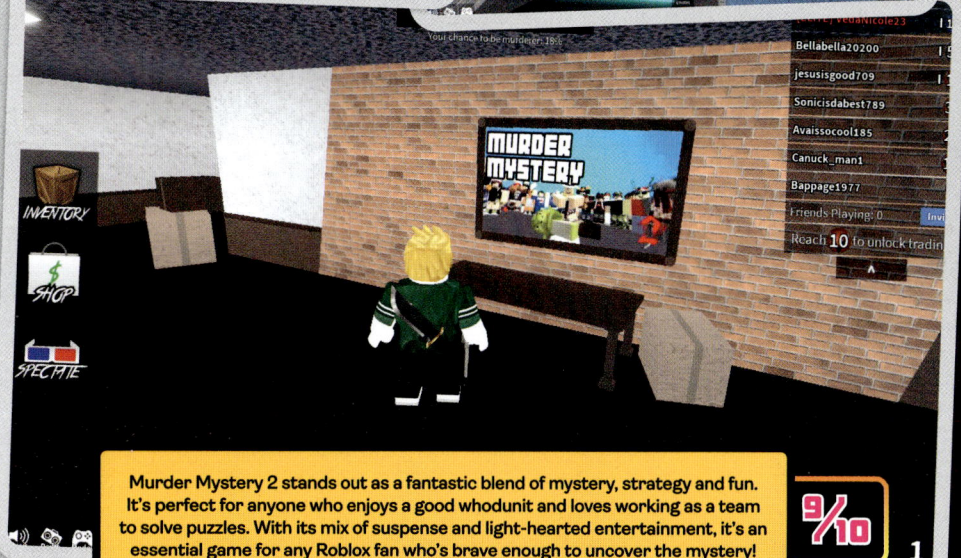

Murder Mystery 2 stands out as a fantastic blend of mystery, strategy and fun. It's perfect for anyone who enjoys a good whodunit and loves working as a team to solve puzzles. With its mix of suspense and light-hearted entertainment, it's an essential game for any Roblox fan who's brave enough to uncover the mystery!

9/10

GAMESWARRIOR VERDICT

ACTION GAMES

Roblox offers a dazzling range of action-packed experiences that will keep you on the edge of your seat! Whether you're engaging in high-intensity combat, navigating challenging obstacle courses, or taking on daring missions, action games on Roblox are designed to deliver non-stop adrenaline and excitement. Let's dive into what makes these fast-paced adventures so captivating.

WHAT DO YOU DO IN ACTION GAMES?

You jump right into the thick of the action! In these games, you're expected to dodge obstacles, outmaneuver opponents and master precise timing in both solo and multiplayer scenarios. Whether you're embarking on daring missions, battling hordes of enemies, or competing against friends in fast-paced challenges, every moment is an opportunity to push your skills to the limit.

WHY ARE ACTION GAMES SO FUN?

The thrill of fast-paced challenges combined with the satisfaction of overcoming demanding obstacles is what makes action games so enjoyable. The blend of intense combat, creative level design and the ever-present adrenaline rush means that every session is a heart-pounding adventure.

HOW DO ACTION GAMES WORK?

Action games on Roblox are built around dynamic gameplay and split-second decision-making. Many test your reflexes through rapid combat, intricate platforming challenges and time-sensitive objectives.

HIDE & SEEK EXTREME

Hide & Seek Extreme offers a frantic and fun twist on the classic game. You can choose to be either a seeker or a hider, navigating imaginative maps filled with clever hiding spots and challenging obstacles. The dynamic gameplay keeps you on your toes, whether you're trying to blend in or frantically searching. The constant tension and thrill of the chase make each round unique.

WHY WE LOVE IT

- The maps offer a fresh take on familiar hiding spots, with interactive elements and hidden passages.

- Whether you're hiding or seeking, the action is non-stop, requiring quick reflexes and split-second decisions.

- Playing with friends adds a whole new level of enjoyment, whether you're coordinating hiding strategies or competing as seekers.

GAMESWARRIOR SAYS

You can earn credits for performing well as a hider or seeker and more are scattered round the map. You can spend them in the shop to buy cosmetic extras!

Hide & Seek Extreme is great for casual gaming. Its simple yet addictive gameplay is perfect for quick bursts of excitement with friends.

7/10

GAMESWARRIOR VERDICT

ATTACK ON TITAN: REVOLUTION

Attack on Titan: Revolution brings the thrilling world of the anime to Roblox. You must swing through the air, taking down Titans with strategic attacks. The game captures the intensity of the original content, offering a challenging experience for fans.

WHY WE LOVE IT

- The recreation of the mechanics is a highlight, allowing you to replicate iconic manoeuvres from the TV shows!

- The scale of the Titans creates a genuine sense of danger, making them formidable opponents. Successfully taking down a Titan feels like a real accomplishment.

- The game encourages teamwork and strategy, as taking down Titans requires co-ordination and skill. This makes victories even more satisfying.

GAMESWARRIOR SAYS

Experiment with different attack strategies and learn Titans' weak points – teamwork is key!

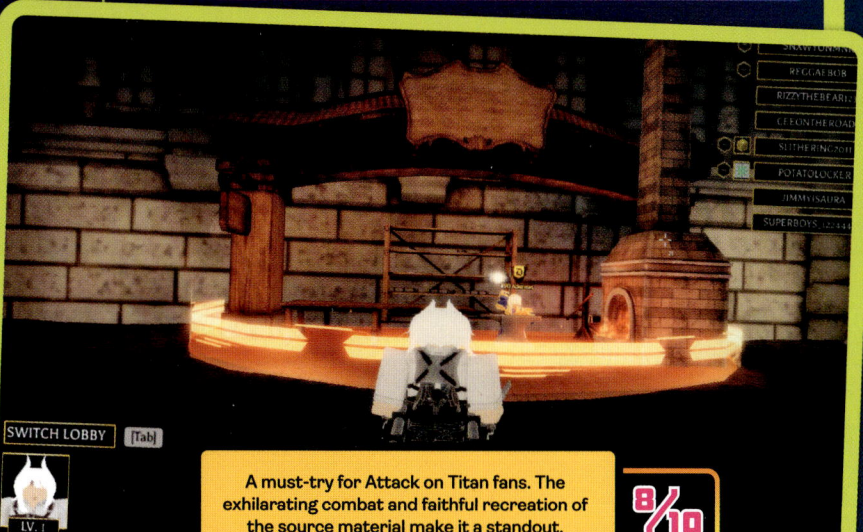

A must-try for Attack on Titan fans. The exhilarating combat and faithful recreation of the source material make it a standout.

8/10

GAMESWARRIOR VERDICT

53

BEDWARS

BedWars offers a strategic and competitive experience, combining PvP combat, resource management and base defence. Teams protect their bed while trying to destroy opponents' beds. It requires careful planning and coordination.

WHY WE LOVE IT

- The blend of player vs player action and base building is engaging, requiring players to balance attack, defence and resource gathering. This keeps the gameplay dynamic.

- Different maps and game modes keep the gameplay fresh, offering varied objectives and team sizes. There's always something new to try.

- The competitive aspect encourages teamwork and skill development. Success requires communication, coordination and adapting to changing circumstances.

GAMESWARRIOR SAYS

Don't underestimate resource management – a well-supplied team has a significant advantage!

HUGE LUCKY BLOCKS INCOMING!

Great for players who enjoy competitive multiplayer games. The strategic depth and fast-paced action make it highly addictive.

8/10

GAMESWARRIOR VERDICT

THE STRONGEST BATTLEGROUNDS

The Strongest Battlegrounds delivers an intense fighting experience. You can choose from a range of characters with unique abilities and fighting styles. The game focuses on fast-paced combat, so you really have to master your character.

WHY WE LOVE IT

- The wide selection of characters offers a variety of playstyles, catering to different preferences. This encourages you to experiment and keeps things fresh!

- The combat system is well-designed, with fluid animations and responsive controls. Landing combos and dodging attacks is a really satisfying feeling.

- The focus on skill means that when you land a win, you really feel like you earned it. It's a game where you have to put the effort in, but it pays off!

GAMESWARRIOR SAYS

Practise with different characters to find your playstyle – mastering abilities is crucial!

A great choice for fighting game fans. The fast-paced action and deep combat system make it thrilling.

7/10

GAMESWARRIOR VERDICT

BLOX FRUITS

Blox Fruits invites you on a quest for mysterious fruits that bestow extraordinary powers. To find them, you'll travel through a vast array of islands, each teeming with challenges and treasures. As you hunt for the fruits, you will need to battle against rival players and formidable foes, all while honing your abilities and mastering a range of combat styles.

The game blends exploration with combat, so every session is thrilling and rewarding. With loads of abilities at your disposal – from hand-to-hand brawling to supernatural attacks – Blox Fruits encourages you to adapt your style to suit each encounter. The progression system allows you to upgrade your character and unlock new skills, rewarding every success. The vibrant community and regular updates further enrich the experience, guaranteeing that there's always something fresh to discover.

GAMESWARRIOR SAYS

As well as earning coins by completing quests, it's worth keeping an eye out for treasure chests on the islands you are visiting to boost your bank balance!

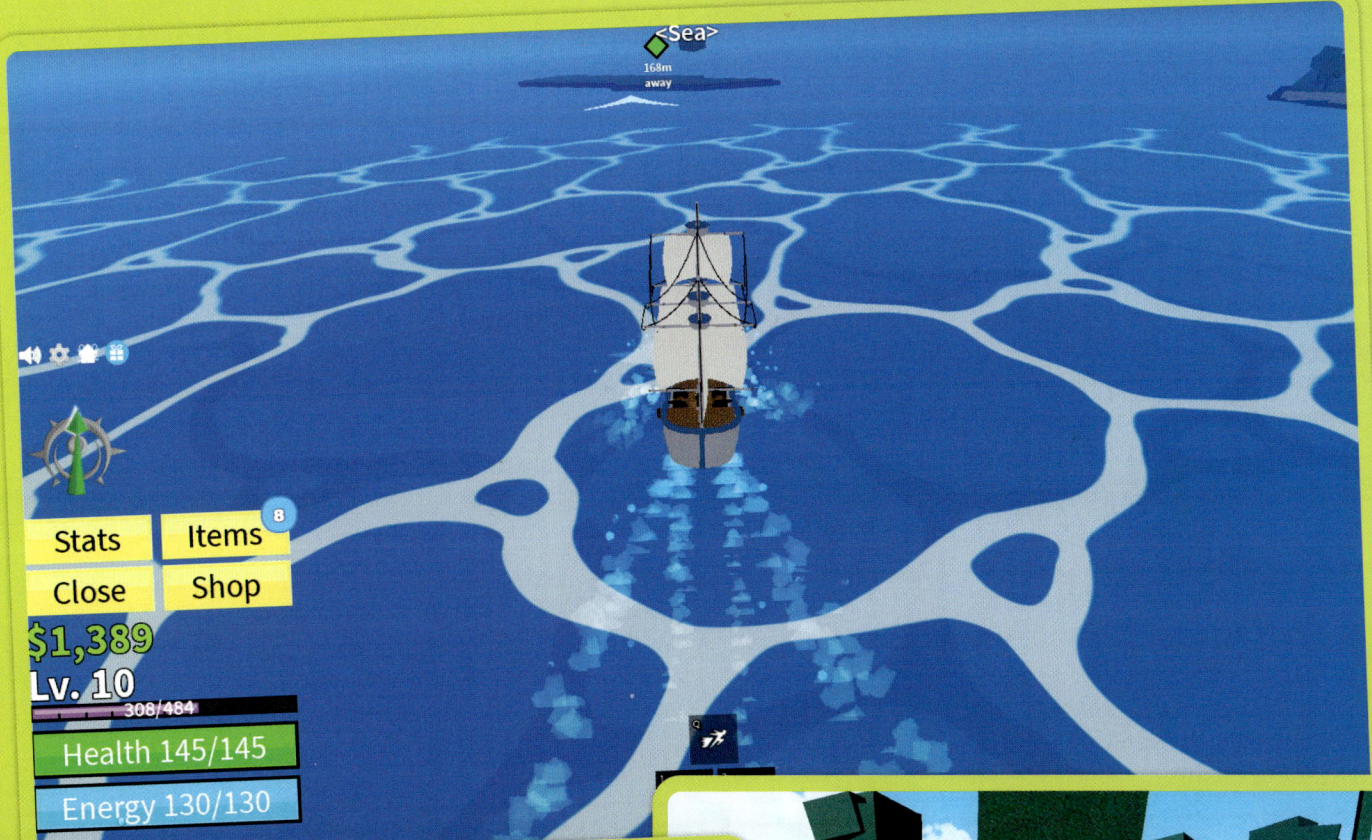

Blox Fruits stands out as a must-play adventure for those who crave action, exploration and a hint of mystery in their Roblox journey.

GAMESWARRIOR VERDICT

10/10

ROLE-PLAYING GAMES

Roblox is the perfect place to step into someone else's shoes and live out incredible stories! Role-playing games (RPGs) allow you to become anything you want – whether it's a medieval knight, a futuristic space explorer, a high school student, or even the mayor of a bustling city. With endless possibilities and immersive experiences, role-playing games on Roblox let your imagination run wild. Let's take a look at what makes them so exciting!

WHAT DO YOU DO IN ROLE-PLAYING GAMES?

You'll be creating stories, making decisions, and exploring detailed worlds. Some RPGs let you take on jobs, earn money, and build homes, while others focus on action-packed adventures, battling enemies and completing challenges. Many encourage social interactions, allowing you to form friendships, join groups and collaborate on exciting missions. Whether you prefer fast-paced action or relaxed storytelling, role-playing games provide endless opportunities.

HOW DO ROLE-PLAYING GAMES WORK?

Role-playing games on Roblox offer a variety of experiences, from structured story-driven adventures to open-ended social hubs. Some games give players quests and objectives, while others are all about interacting with other players and building your own narrative. Many RPGs include in-depth character customisation, letting you choose your appearance, outfits, and even personality traits. Whether you want to follow a set path or carve your own, there's something for everyone.

WHY ARE ROLE-PLAYING GAMES SO FUN?

The freedom to become anyone and do anything is what makes role-playing games so special. Whether you want to be a hero, a villain, or just an everyday citizen, these games let you live out your fantasies in incredible virtual worlds. The ability to connect with friends, create unforgettable moments and shape your own adventures makes role-playing games one of the most exciting and immersive genres on Roblox!

HORDE SLAYER: CONAN

This action-packed game invites you to test your mettle against relentless waves of foes in a gritty, Conan-inspired setting. You assume the role of a formidable warrior, taking on hordes of enemies with skilful melee combat and strategic manoeuvring. The game's dark, atmospheric design and challenging combat keep you constantly on your toes as you push your abilities to the limit.

GAMESWARRIOR SAYS

Successful missions earn you loot, which you can use to buy weapons and armour to help you head into battle with more dangerous opponents!

WHY WE LOVE IT

• The intense, fast-paced combat offers a thrilling test of reflexes and strategy.

• Its immersive, gritty environment draws you into a world where every battle feels hard-earned.

• The ever-increasing challenge ensures that each encounter remains fresh and engaging.

If you enjoy testing your combat skills in a dark, relentless environment, this game is a must-try.

8/10

GAMESWARRIOR VERDICT

ELEMENTAL BATTLEGROUNDS

Elemental Battlegrounds challenges you to master the forces of nature in competitive combat. You do this by harnessing elemental powers and stepping into dynamic arenas where strategy and skill are key. The game encourages you to experiment with different elemental abilities while engaging in fast-paced battles that test your tactical thinking and reflexes.

GAMESWARRIOR SAYS

The more experience you gain in the game, the more powers and spells you unlock – and you can shape the strengths and weaknesses of your avatar!

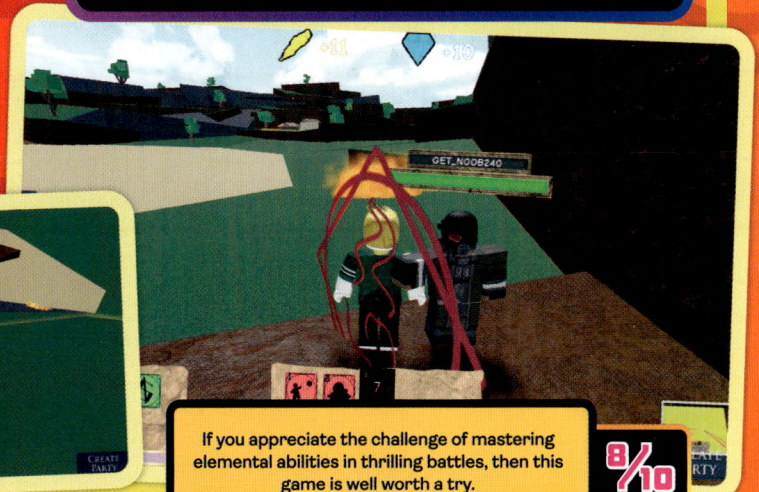

WHY WE LOVE IT

• The unique focus on elemental powers offers a fresh twist on traditional combat.

• Its dynamic arenas ensure that every match feels varied and engaging.

• The blend of role-playing and competitive action invites creative strategies and personal expression.

If you appreciate the challenge of mastering elemental abilities in thrilling battles, then this game is well worth a try.

8/10

GAMESWARRIOR VERDICT

THE WILD WEST

Yee-haw! Saddle up cowboys and cowgirls because this game is going to transport you straight to the Wild West! This themed RPG gives you the chance to create your own adventures at the frontier!

WHY WE LOVE IT

- There's so much choice in what to do – you can be an outlaw, a sheriff, a miner or a hunter to make your money!

- You can accessorise your avatar to develop your karaoke persona!

- It's a friendly community where players cheer each other on and support performances.

GAMESWARRIOR SAYS

RPGs can be quite overwhelming to start with, so The Wild West has a safe zone, where your character can't be hurt, while you figure out the basics of the game and how you'd like to play it.

A rootin'-tootin' roleplaying romp! The Wild West lets you live out cowboy dreams with freedom, flair and fun, in a supportive community.

8/10

GAMESWARRIOR VERDICT

DYSTOVIA

Dystovia is a role-playing game on Roblox that invites you into a uniquely immersive dystopian setting. In this game, you step into a world where the familiar rules of everyday life are turned on their head, offering you a canvas to create your own narrative. The focus is on delivering engaging role-play experiences that let you develop your character, interact with others and explore a society that challenges conventional expectations. Its design encourages you to think creatively and collaborate, making every session a fresh adventure in a setting that is both reflective and imaginative.

WHY WE LOVE IT

- The atmospheric design creates a perfect backdrop for deep role-playing.

- Over 200 pieces of equipment mean that there are loads of ways to customise your character!

- It's a hugely popular game with a very active community, so there are regular updates and there's always something new happening!

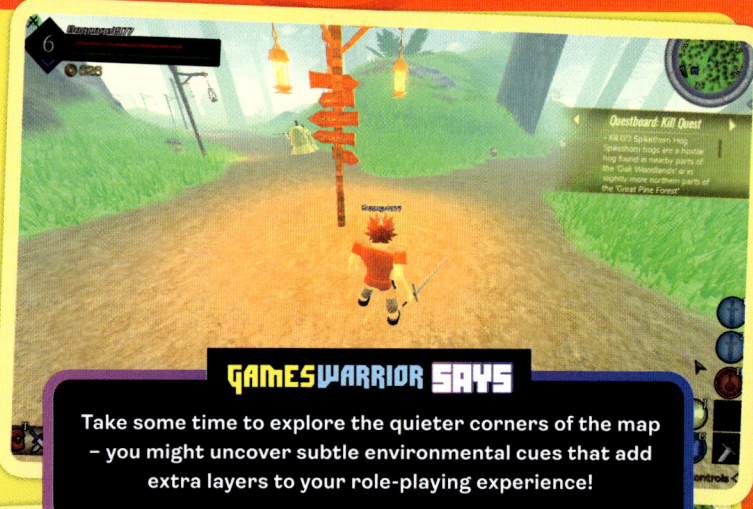

GAMESWARRIOR SAYS

Take some time to explore the quieter corners of the map – you might uncover subtle environmental cues that add extra layers to your role-playing experience!

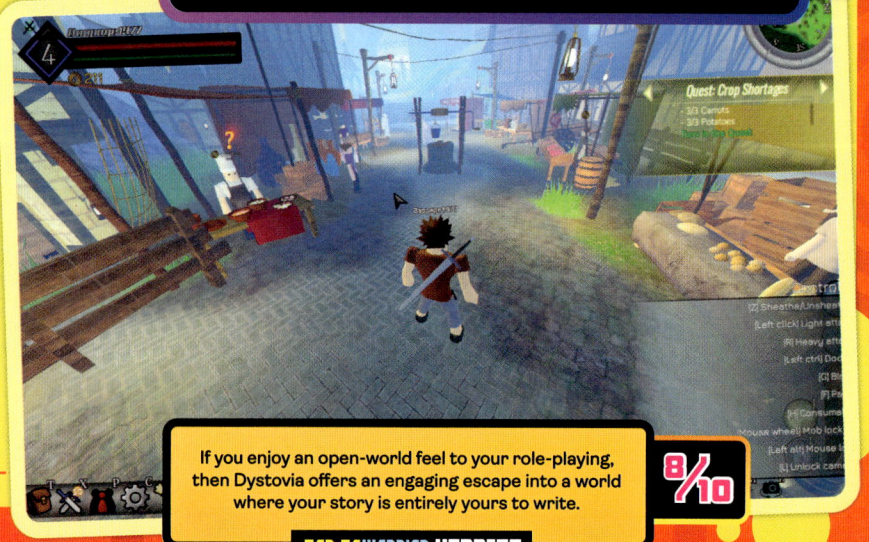

If you enjoy an open-world feel to your role-playing, then Dystovia offers an engaging escape into a world where your story is entirely yours to write.

8/10

GAMESWARRIOR VERDICT

BROOKHAVEN

Brookhaven is one of the premier role-playing experiences on Roblox, inviting you to immerse yourself in a sprawling suburban world where your virtual life is entirely your own. In this expansive and ever-evolving environment, you are free to craft your narrative – whether that means living a cosy life at home, venturing out on exciting journeys with friends, or simply exploring a community designed with an impressive attention to detail. Every element, from the charming houses to the sleek vehicles, is meticulously crafted to provide you with an authentic slice of modern living.

The game's open-ended design is its greatest strength, offering a blank canvas where you can explore, create and interact at your own pace. Without strict objectives or time limits, Brookhaven encourages you to embrace a sense of freedom and creativity, tailoring your experiences to suit your mood and imagination. The social aspect is equally engaging, as you join a vibrant community of role-players who are all adding their own stories to the mix, making each visit a new adventure.

GAMESWARRIOR SAYS

One of the most enjoyable aspects of Brookhaven is building your own home – starting with something small like a motel room before moving on to bigger and better things!

Brookhaven stands as a landmark in Roblox role-playing, seamlessly blending simplicity with boundless opportunities for creative expression. If you value the freedom to shape your own story in a welcoming and dynamic environment, then Brookhaven is an essential experience.

GAMESWARRIOR VERDICT

10/10

SPORTS GAMES

Roblox is a fantastic place to experience the thrill of sports! From classic games like football and basketball to more unique experiences, Roblox offers a great range of sports games to get your adrenaline pumping. Let's dive in and see what the world of Roblox sports has to offer!

WHAT DO YOU DO IN SPORTS GAMES?

You'll be competing against other players (or sometimes AI opponents), trying to score points, win matches and ultimately become the best. Some games focus on teamwork, requiring coordination and communication to succeed, while others are more individualistic, testing your skills and reflexes. Many offer customisation options, letting you personalise your avatar's appearance and choose from a range of equipment.

HOW DO SPORTS GAMES WORK?

Roblox sports games vary in their approach. Some aim for realistic simulations, meticulously recreating the physics and strategies of real-world sports, while others offer a more arcade-like experience, prioritising fun and fast-paced action over realism. Most involve controlling an avatar and participating in matches or competitions. Many games feature progression systems, allowing you to improve your skills, unlock new abilities, or acquire better equipment as you play.

WHY ARE SPORTS GAMES SO FUN?

The thrill of competition, the satisfaction of mastering a skill and the social aspect of playing with friends are all key to the appeal of sports games. Roblox adds its own twist with creative game modes, unique environments, and often over-the-top physics, making for a fresh and exciting take on familiar sports. The ability to connect with friends and compete in a virtual world adds another layer of enjoyment.

BASKETBALL LEGENDS

Basketball Legends offers a fast-paced and energetic take on one of the world's most popular sports. It's less about meticulously recreating the nuances of professional basketball and more about delivering an adrenaline-pumping experience where spectacular dunks, gravity-defying leaps, and special abilities take centre stage.

WHY WE LOVE IT

- Fast-paced and action-packed gameplay keeps you on the edge of your seat.

- The focus on trick shots, dunks and special abilities makes for exciting and unpredictable matches.

- Regular updates with new content and features, including maps, characters, and game modes, ensure the experience stays fresh and engaging.

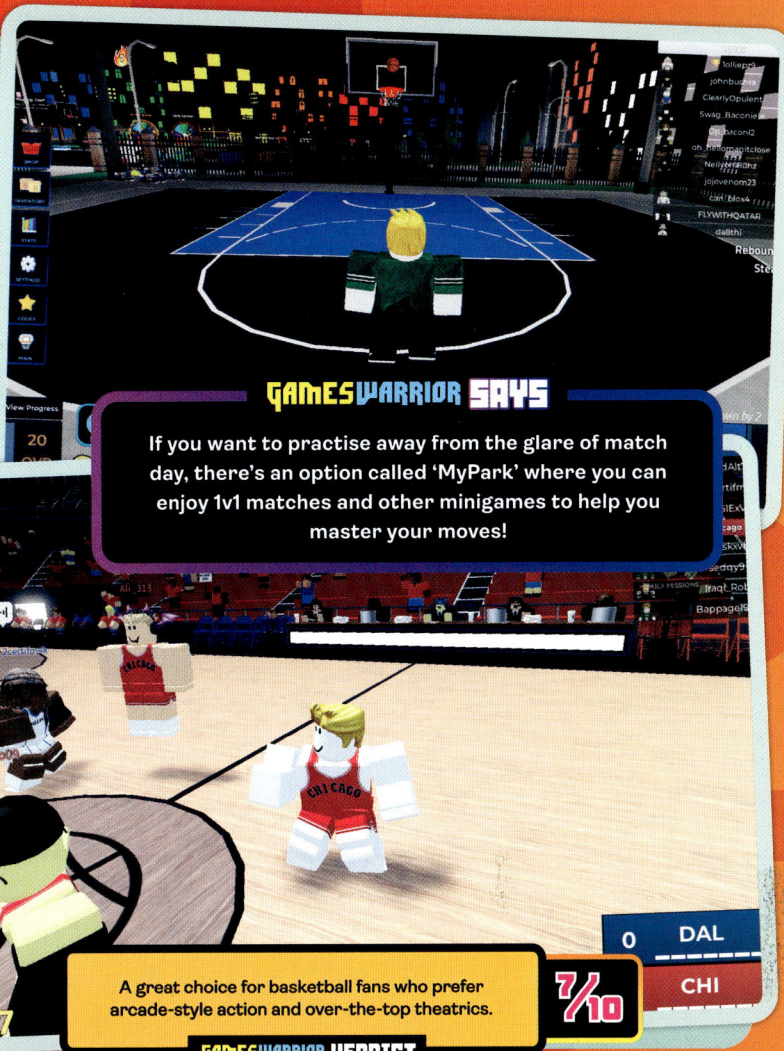

GAMESWARRIOR SAYS

If you want to practise away from the glare of match day, there's an option called 'MyPark' where you can enjoy 1v1 matches and other minigames to help you master your moves!

A great choice for basketball fans who prefer arcade-style action and over-the-top theatrics.

7/10

GAMESWARRIOR VERDICT

SUPER GOLF!

Super Golf! brings a delightfully chaotic brand of golf to Roblox. Forget pristine greens and hushed concentration; this is about outlandish courses, crazy power-ups, and friendly competition. Imagine teeing off across floating islands, dodging giant windmills and curving your ball around impossible obstacles. That's Super Golf!

WHY WE LOVE IT

- From volcanic landscapes to candy wonderlands, the level design is inventive and hilarious. Each course offers unique challenges and surprises.

- Super boosts, sticky balls, and ball teleportation add strategic depth (and total chaos!).

- Super Golf! shines with friends. Shared laughter and friendly rivalry navigating wacky courses make it truly enjoyable.

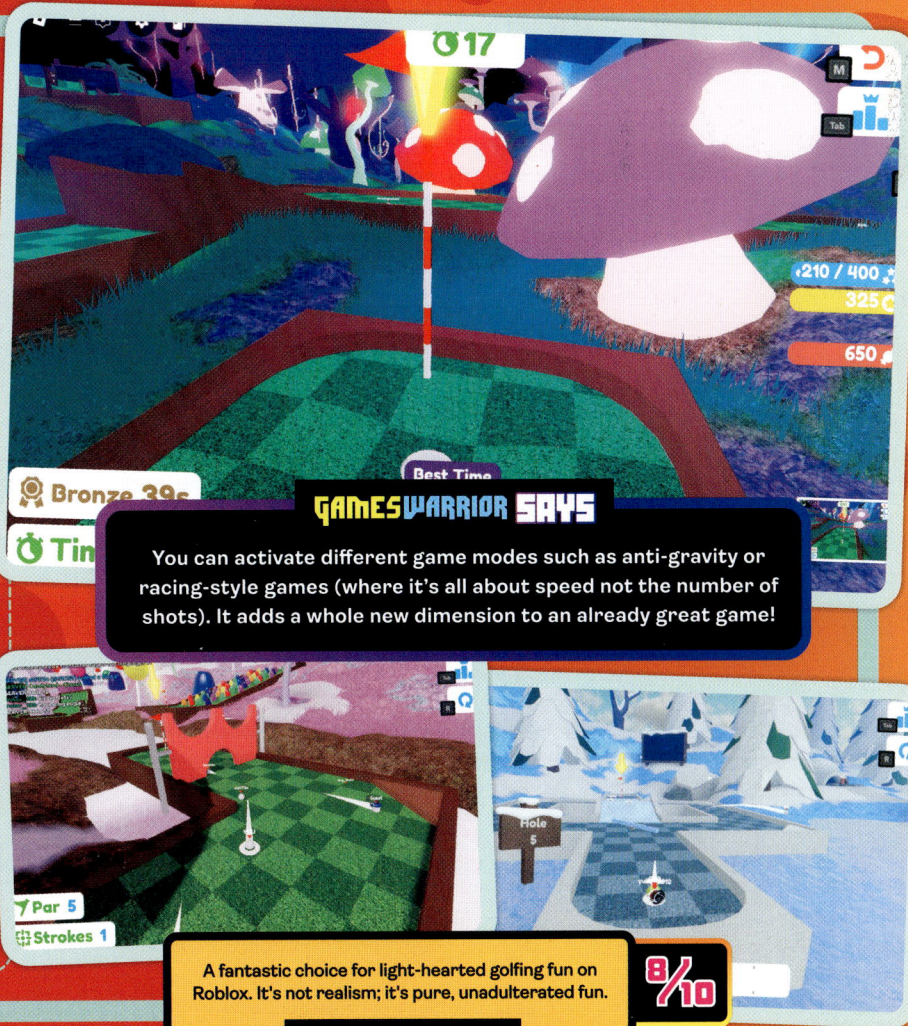

GAMESWARRIOR SAYS

You can activate different game modes such as anti-gravity or racing-style games (where it's all about speed not the number of shots). It adds a whole new dimension to an already great game!

A fantastic choice for light-hearted golfing fun on Roblox. It's not realism; it's pure, unadulterated fun.

8/10

GAMESWARRIOR VERDICT

HOME RUN SIMULATOR

Home Run Simulator captures the simple pleasure of hitting towering home runs in a Roblox environment. Earn coins, boost your stats and hit some home runs! It's simple gameplay at its very best!

WHY WE LOVE IT

- Perfect for short bursts of gaming, this title doesn't require a huge time commitment.

- Combining different bats and balls can see you hitting the ball further and further!

- You can compete in a championship which offers a slightly different style of gameplay!

GAMESWARRIOR SAYS

As you improve, you can unlock areas further away from the fence – head into the parking lot to see if you can score a home run from there, or even from the MOON!

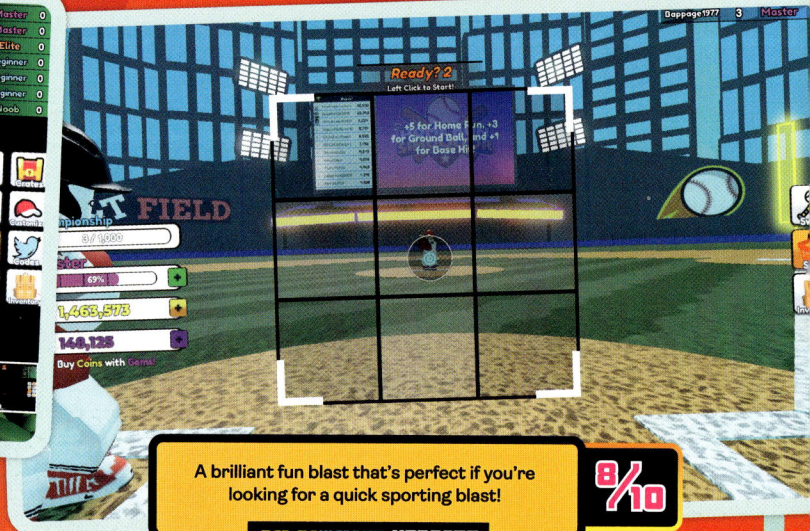

A brilliant fun blast that's perfect if you're looking for a quick sporting blast!

8/10

GAMESWARRIOR VERDICT

WIMBLEWORLD TENNIS

An awesome take on tennis, based on the home of the sport itself! You can enter tournaments, play against others in one-off matches, or take on some truly bonkers mini-games!

GAMESWARRIOR SAYS

If you look up at the big screens on the outside of the stadium, they are showing highlights from real previous Wimbledon matches – how cool is that?!

WHY WE LOVE IT

- It's easy to pick up and play, with simple controls making everything easy.

- Quirky touches such as collecting pigeons to earn rewards are guaranteed to put a smile on your face!

- It's well maintained and busy – there's always someone to play against if you want to!

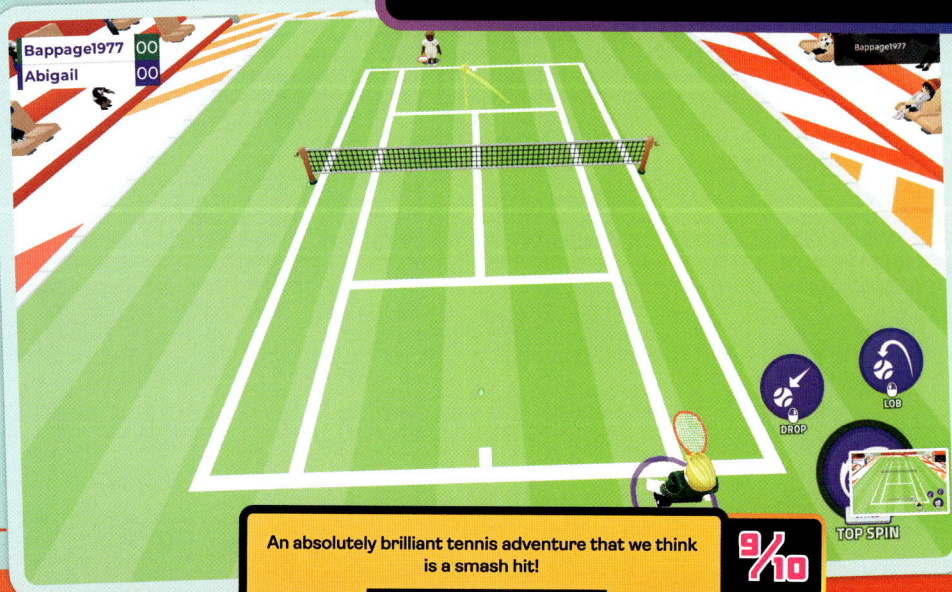

An absolutely brilliant tennis adventure that we think is a smash hit!

9/10

GAMESWARRIOR VERDICT

SUPER LEAGUE SOCCER

Super League Soccer is a 7 v 7 football simulation that sees you drop into a match with six teammates and take on another side. It's easy to pick up the basics and you'll soon get the hang of slide tackling, passing and shooting!

It can sometimes take a while to gel with new teammates in the game, but it's working together as a group that really makes the game stand out. It also gets regular updates, so when issues do crop up they're quickly ironed out – another win!

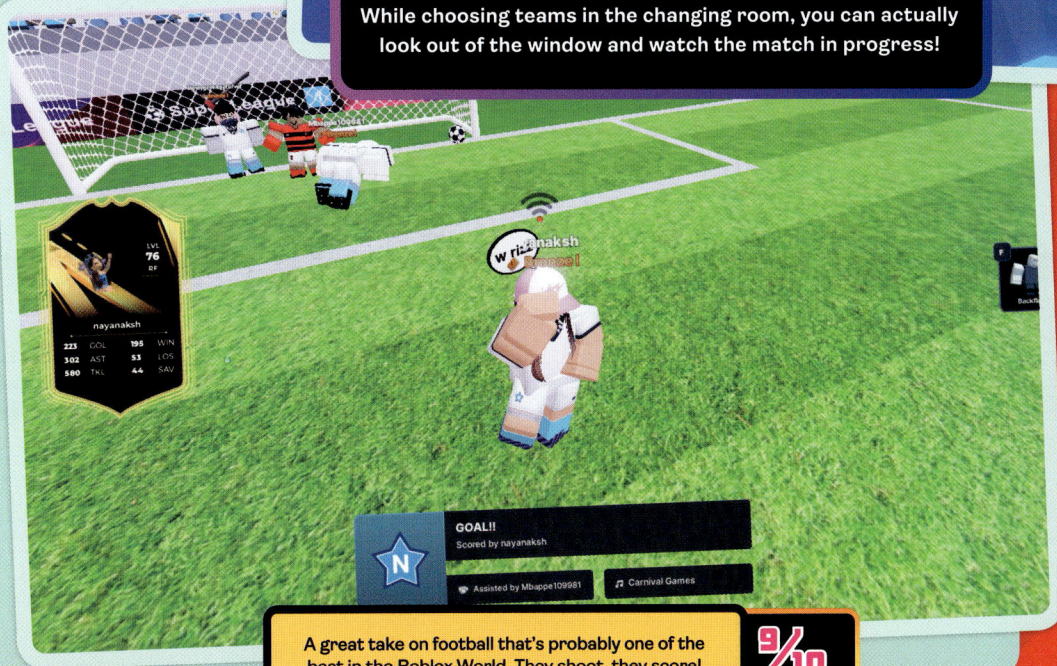

MUSICAL EXPERIENCES

Roblox isn't just about fast-paced sports or thrilling adventures – it's also home to some truly fantastic musical experiences! Whether you want to play instruments, perform in front of a crowd, or even build your own music empire, Roblox has a rhythm-filled world waiting for you. Let's dive in and see what musical experiences Roblox has to offer!

WHAT DO YOU DO IN MUSICAL EXPERIENCES?

You'll be playing, creating, or performing music! Some games allow you to compete against others in rhythm challenges, while others encourage collaboration, letting you form bands, sing duets, or compose tunes together. Many experiences offer personalisation options, so you can create your own unique musical style, dress up for performances, or even design your own virtual instruments.

WHY ARE MUSICAL EXPERIENCES SO FUN?

Music is an incredible way to express yourself, and Roblox makes it even more exciting by adding interactive elements, creative twists, and social features. Whether you're playing a virtual drum kit, stepping into a Broadway musical, or rocking out in a karaoke battle, the thrill of making music is something truly special. Plus, the ability to share these experiences with friends makes them even more enjoyable!

HOW DO MUSICAL EXPERIENCES WORK?

Roblox musical experiences come in all shapes and sizes. Some focus on instrument simulation, letting you play notes and perform songs, while others allow you to step into the shoes of a performer or a music producer. Some games offer rhythm-based challenges, testing your timing and reflexes, while others are about creativity, giving you tools to compose and share your own tracks. Whether you're looking to jam with friends or create the next chart-topping hit, there's a musical experience for you.

DIGITAL PIANO

This is perfection for piano players! Digital Piano is really easy to get into, with lots of different options and plenty of room for practise and improvement. A great way to spend some time tinkling the ivories. We mean keys. You knew what we meant!

WHY WE LOVE IT

• You can choose from different types of rooms, so you can play somewhere that suits you.

• It's super easy to choose between different types of sound, so it's more like playing a keyboard than a piano – harpsichord, anyone?

• You can pre-program difficult sections of notes so that they will play automatically, making it easier to put together a long piece of music without mistakes!

GAMESWARRIOR SAYS
If you are happy to pay for the privilege, you can take a turn on the grand piano itself – though be warned, people will be listening!!

Lots of fun to be had here even if you've never played the piano before. We couldn't tear ourselves away!

GAMESWARRIOR VERDICT
8/10

WICKED RP

Step into the film that everyone went wild for back in November 2024 with Wicked RP, a Roblox experience that lets you immerse yourself in the magic of Oz.

WHY WE LOVE IT

• The detailed game world is brilliantly captured – you'll feel like you're really there!

• You can play in different roles and take on different sub quests – there's always something new to try!

• The interactive elements, like costume changes and stage effects, make every performance feel unique.

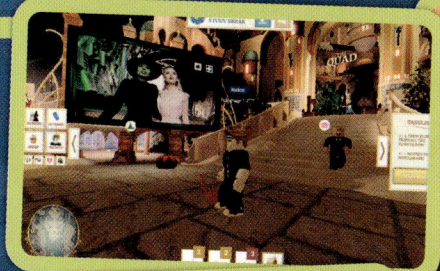

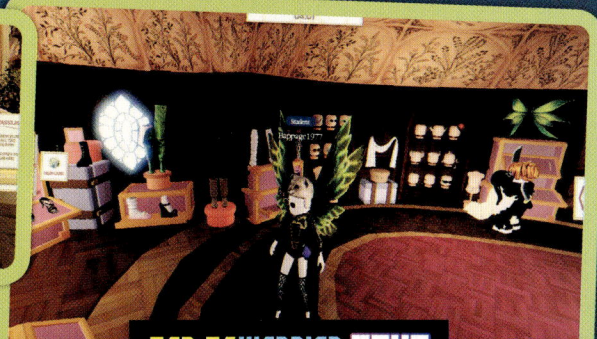

GAMESWARRIOR SAYS
Check out the fashion minigame – you're set a challenge to dress in a certain style, and a winner is chosen from those who take part after a catwalk show!

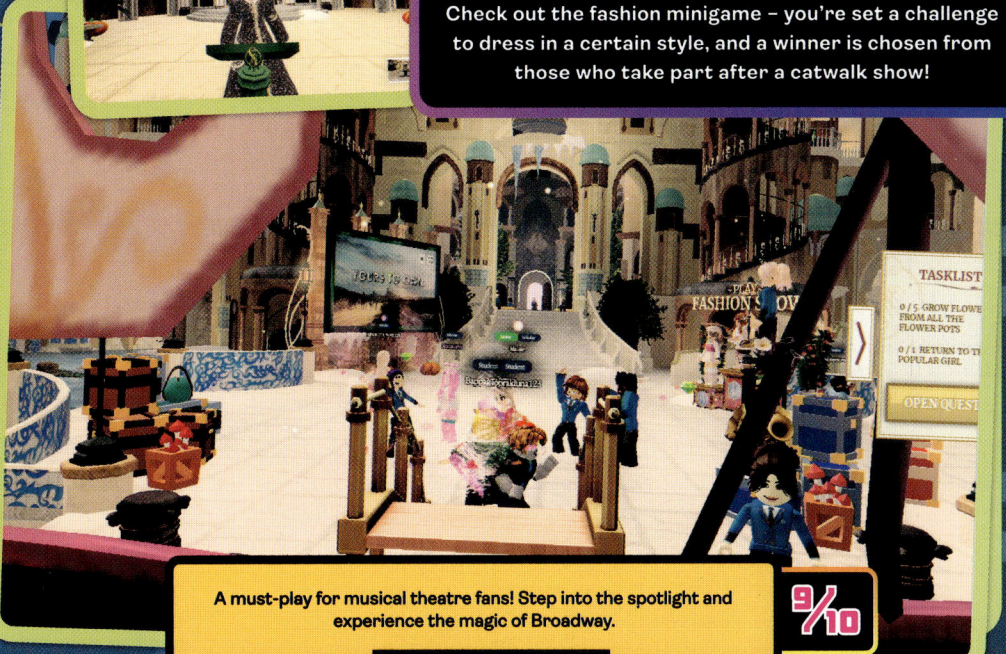

A must-play for musical theatre fans! Step into the spotlight and experience the magic of Broadway.

GAMESWARRIOR VERDICT
9/10

DAN'S KARAOKE

Love singing? Dan's Karaoke is the perfect place to show off your vocal skills. Join a lobby, pick your favourite song, and take the stage in front of an audience of other players.

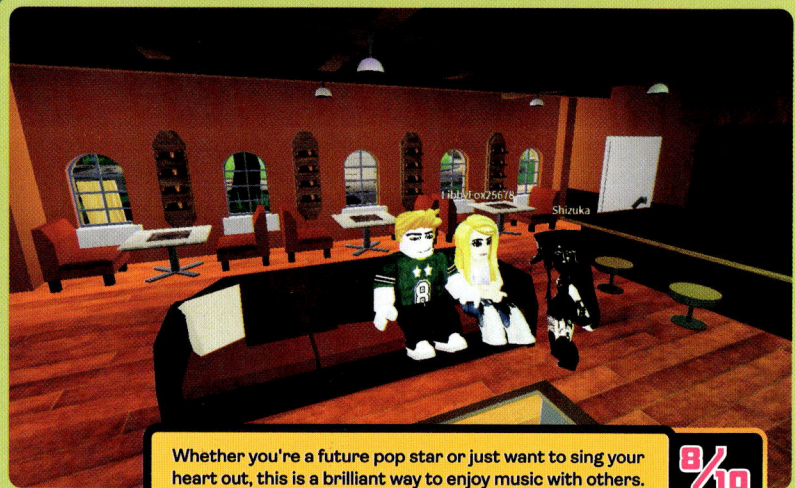

WHY WE LOVE IT

- It has a massive song library, so there's always something to sing – and content is driven by users so it's always current

- You can accessorise your avatar to develop your karaoke persona!

- The community is friendly and players cheer each other on and support performances.

Whether you're a future pop star or just want to sing your heart out, this is a brilliant way to enjoy music with others. **8/10**

GAMESWARRIOR VERDICT

SINGERS TYCOON

Ever wanted to run your own music empire? Singers Tycoon lets you develop a band, adding more members and extra on-stage effects as you work your way towards the top of the charts.

WHY WE LOVE IT

- It's a simple and enjoyable tycoon-style game.

- The better you get, the more money you make from fans.

- You have to make difficult choices between improving your current band or adding new aspects to your performances!

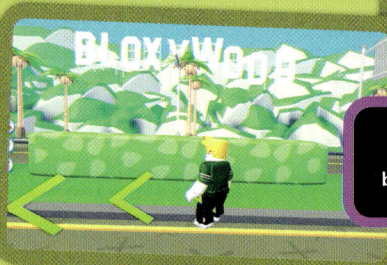

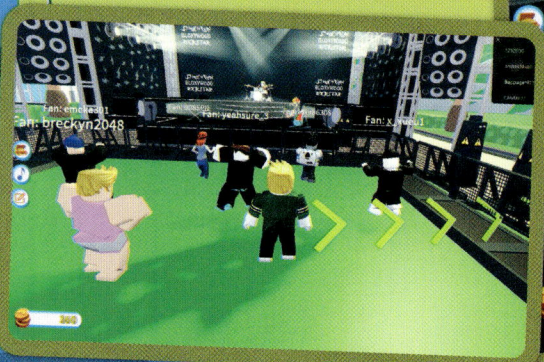

A great way to build your own band – it's really satisfying to see them grow from playing to an empty room to becoming ROCK GODS! **9/10**

GAMESWARRIOR VERDICT

BEATMERGER

BeatMerger is a fantastic piece of music-making software in the Roblox world that allows you to make your own music using in-game instruments and beats. It pulls off the very difficult achievement of being easy for beginners to pick up while having enough features and depth to allow expert users to really push what they are capable of.

You can have five different instruments (or 'tracks') in a song (you can have up to seven if you pay for a GamePass, but you don't really need the extra to start with at least). You can set the tempo and the notes in each section to build your tune and loop sections to build your own piece of music.

When you're done, you can even move into the multiplayer version of the game, where multiple people can work on the track at once!

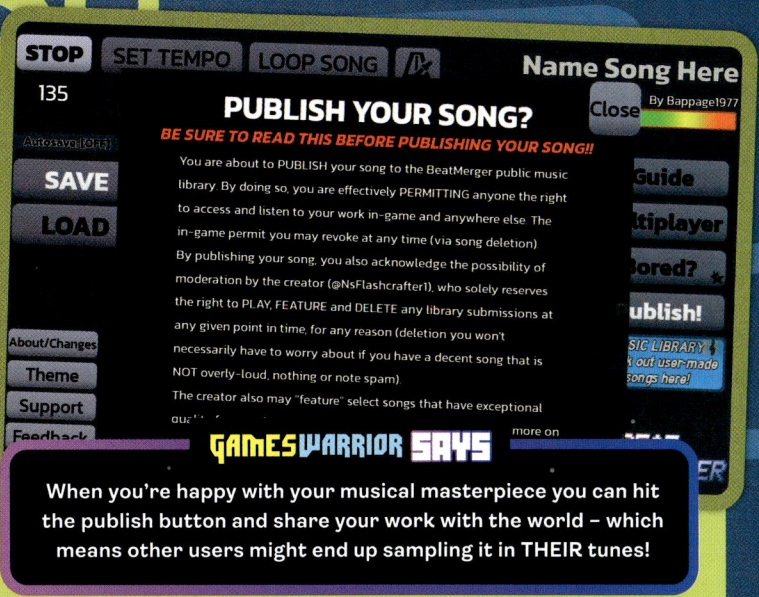

PUBLISH YOUR SONG?

BE SURE TO READ THIS BEFORE PUBLISHING YOUR SONG!!

You are about to PUBLISH your song to the BeatMerger public music library. By doing so, you are effectively PERMITTING anyone the right to access and listen to your work in-game and anywhere else. The in-game permit you may revoke at any time (via song deletion)

By publishing your song, you also acknowledge the possibility of moderation by the creator (@NsFlashcrafter1), who solely reserves the right to PLAY, FEATURE and DELETE any library submissions at any given point in time, for any reason (deletion you won't necessarily have to worry about if you have a decent song that is NOT overly-loud, nothing or note spam).

The creator also may "feature" select songs that have exceptional quality

GAMESWARRIOR SAYS

When you're happy with your musical masterpiece you can hit the publish button and share your work with the world – which means other users might end up sampling it in THEIR tunes!

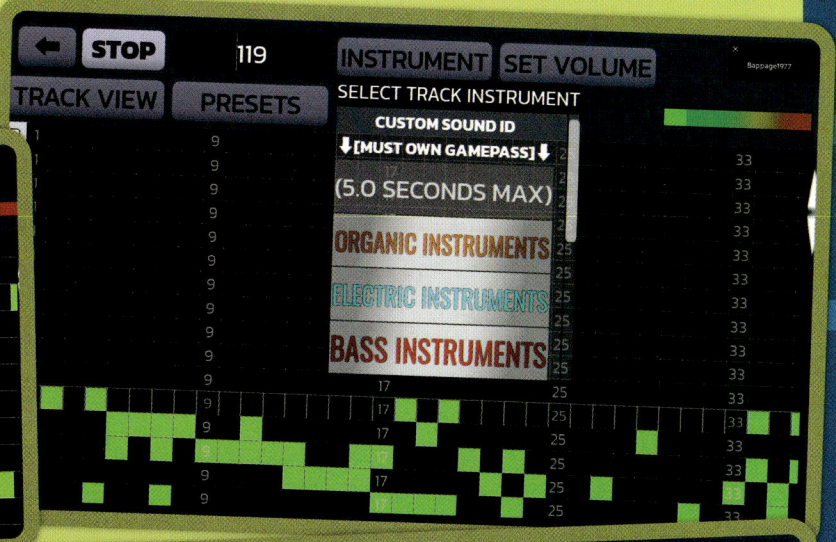

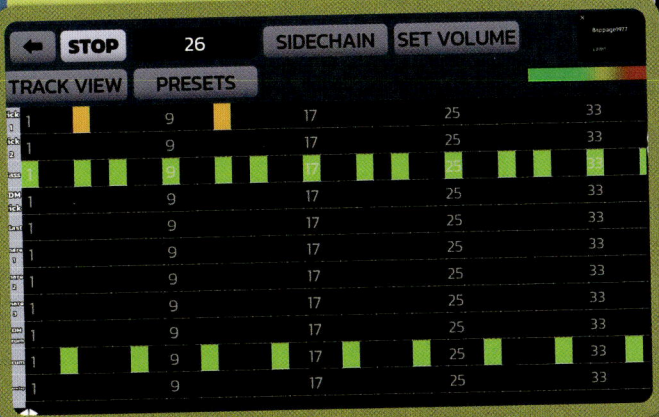

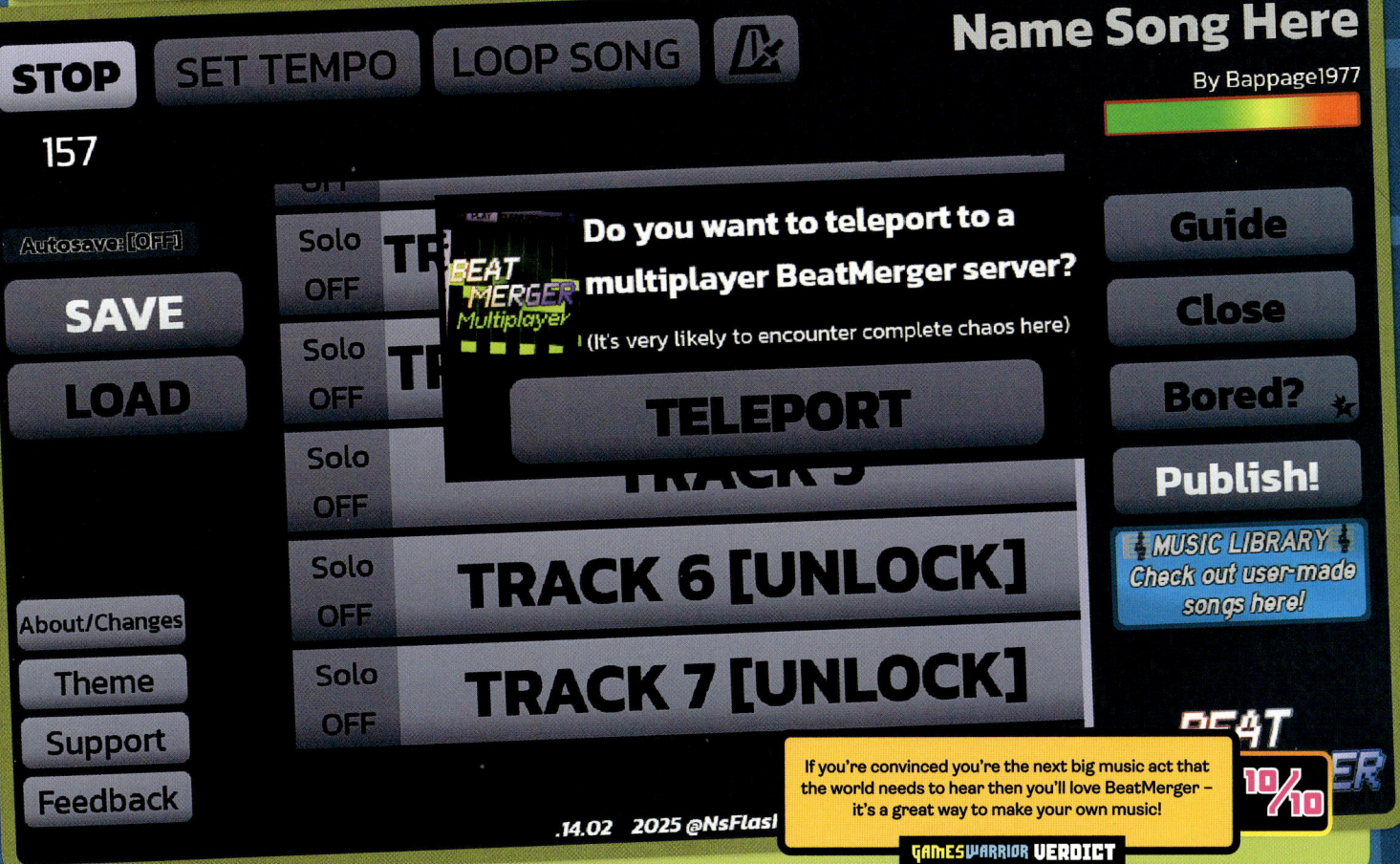

Do you want to teleport to a multiplayer BeatMerger server?

(It's very likely to encounter complete chaos here)

TELEPORT

TRACK 6 [UNLOCK]

TRACK 7 [UNLOCK]

If you're convinced you're the next big music act that the world needs to hear then you'll love BeatMerger – it's a great way to make your own music!

GAMESWARRIOR VERDICT

10/10

RECREATIONS & TRIBUTES

Roblox is more than just a platform for original creations – it's a vibrant space where creative minds pay homage to some of the most iconic games from beyond its own universe. From battle royale adventures reminiscent of Fortnite to speed-based challenges echoing the high-velocity thrills of Sonic the Hedgehog, inventive developers have ingeniously recreated elements of these beloved titles within Roblox. These tributes let you experience familiar gameplay mechanics reimagined with a unique, community-driven twist, ensuring that every session is both a nod to nostalgia and a fresh, exciting adventure.

HOW DO THESE RECREATED GAMES WORK?

Developers harness the powerful building tools of Roblox to capture the essence of the original games, blending recognised mechanics with innovative new features. Whether you're engaging in competitive shootouts in a Fortnite-inspired battle royale or sprinting through intricately designed courses that recall Sonic's speedy escapades, each recreation is carefully crafted to maintain the spirit of its source while offering an experience that's distinctly Roblox.

WHAT DO YOU DO IN THESE RECREATED GAMES?

You dive into worlds where classic game elements are given a new lease of life. Step into a battle royale arena that mirrors the intensity of Fortnite, or race through vibrant, obstacle-filled landscapes that pay tribute to Sonic's iconic speed and agility. The joy lies in reliving the excitement of well-known titles while exploring reinterpreted environments that invite you to test your skills, collaborate with friends, and enjoy a fresh perspective on familiar challenges.

WHY ARE THESE RECREATIONS SO FUN?

They offer the perfect blend of nostalgia and innovation. By transforming your favourite games into uniquely Roblox experiences, developers allow you to revisit cherished gameplay in a novel setting. The combination of time-honoured mechanics and imaginative twists means you get the best of both worlds – the comfort of the classics and the thrill of new, engaging experiences that only Roblox can deliver.

CLASSIC SONIC SIMULATOR

Love the old-school Sonic games? Classic Sonic Simulator lets you relive the fast-paced, loop-de-loop action of the original Sonic the Hedgehog right inside Roblox! You can dash through familiar zones, jump over obstacles and even play as different characters from the Sonic universe. Plus, you can create and share your own custom Sonic levels!

WHY WE LOVE IT

- Feels just like the original Sonic games, with smooth movement and fun platforming.

- Loads of playable characters to unlock and try out.

- The level editor means endless creative possibilities!

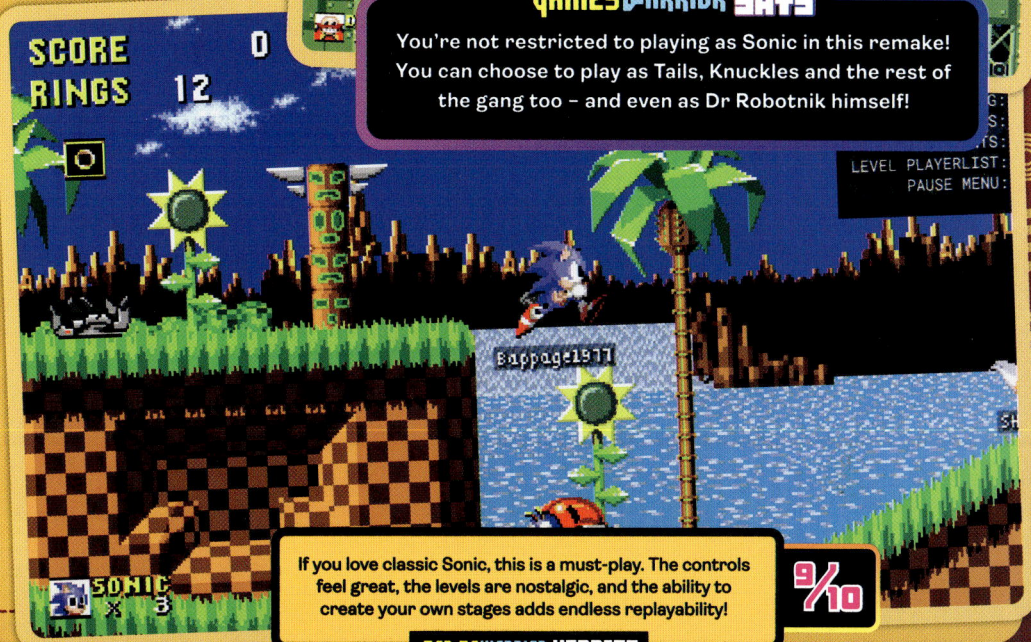

GAMESWARRIOR SAYS

You're not restricted to playing as Sonic in this remake! You can choose to play as Tails, Knuckles and the rest of the gang too – and even as Dr Robotnik himself!

If you love classic Sonic, this is a must-play. The controls feel great, the levels are nostalgic, and the ability to create your own stages adds endless replayability!

9/10

GAMESWARRIOR VERDICT

ROBOT 64 (SUPER MARIO 64)

This 3D platformer has been a huge favourite on Roblox since it first landed WAAAAY back in 2018. It draws very heavy inspiration from Super Mario 64, and puts you in the role of Beebo, a robot who must navigate a very Mario-like world!

WHY WE LOVE IT

- There are a good variety of different mission types, from standard platforming challenges to more open-ended quests.

- Fantastic attention to detail means that even the little details are covered – it really feels like you're playing Mario 64.

- The controls are smooth and responsive, making tricky jumps and exploration feel fun rather than frustrating.

GAMESWARRIOR SAYS

Once you've got the hang of it, you can even head to the level hub and create your own levels in the game to play – and you can allow others to play them too!

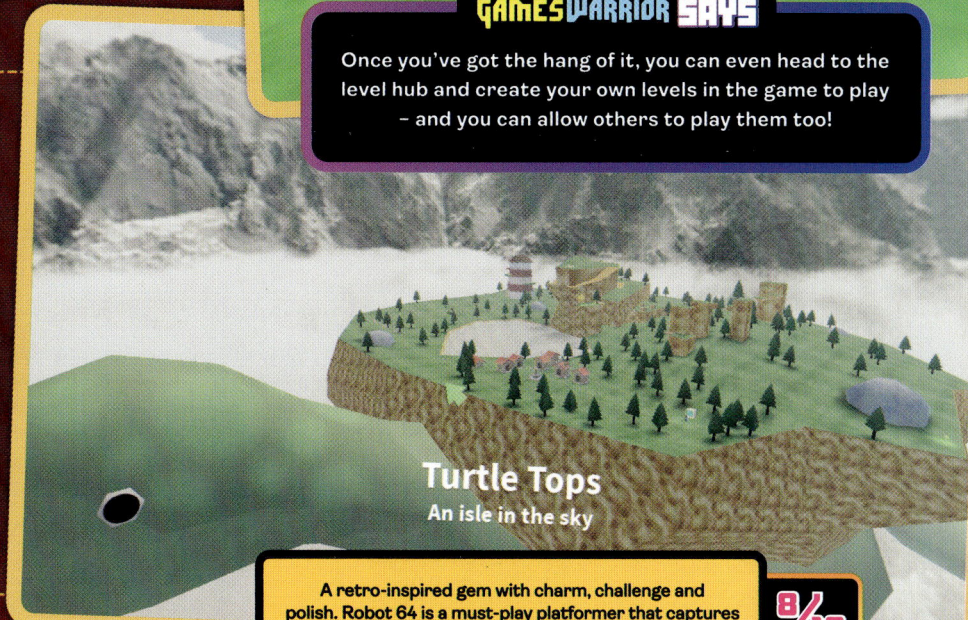

Turtle Tops
An isle in the sky

A retro-inspired gem with charm, challenge and polish. Robot 64 is a must-play platformer that captures the spirit of Mario with robotic flair!

8/10

GAMESWARRIOR VERDICT

69

Q-CLASH (OVERWATCH)

Q-Clash is heavily inspired by Overwatch, so is a great title to play if you're a fan of the original. It's a fast-paced, team-based shooter that throws you into the thick of the action. Q-Clash is a vibrant and chaotic experience, with a diverse range of characters to choose from, and one that Overwatch fans in particular will love!

WHY WE LOVE IT

- There is a wide variety of heroes, each with their own unique abilities and playstyles, just like Overwatch.

- The maps are well-designed and offer plenty of opportunities for strategic gameplay.

- It's surprisingly polished for a Roblox game, with smooth performance and regular updates.

GAMESWARRIOR SAYS

Just like on Overwatch, you can build and place items that can help you surprise your opponents and gain a strategic advantage!

A colourful, chaotic blast! Q-Clash delivers slick team-based action with plenty of strategy—perfect for Overwatch fans looking for fun on Roblox.

9/10

GAMESWARRIOR VERDICT

ROOM (DOOM)

RooM delivers a nostalgic blast from the past with its fast-paced, demon-slaying action. It's a clear homage to the classic Doom games, capturing the frantic energy and visceral combat that made the originals so iconic. Prepare for hordes of enemies and a healthy dose of pixelated gore!

WHY WE LOVE IT

- All your favourite Doom weapons are here, from the shotgun to the monster-slaying BFG.

- The level design faithfully recreates the claustrophobic corridors and hidden secrets of the original games.

- It brilliantly captures the intensity of the original – your heart will be pounding when the action heats up!

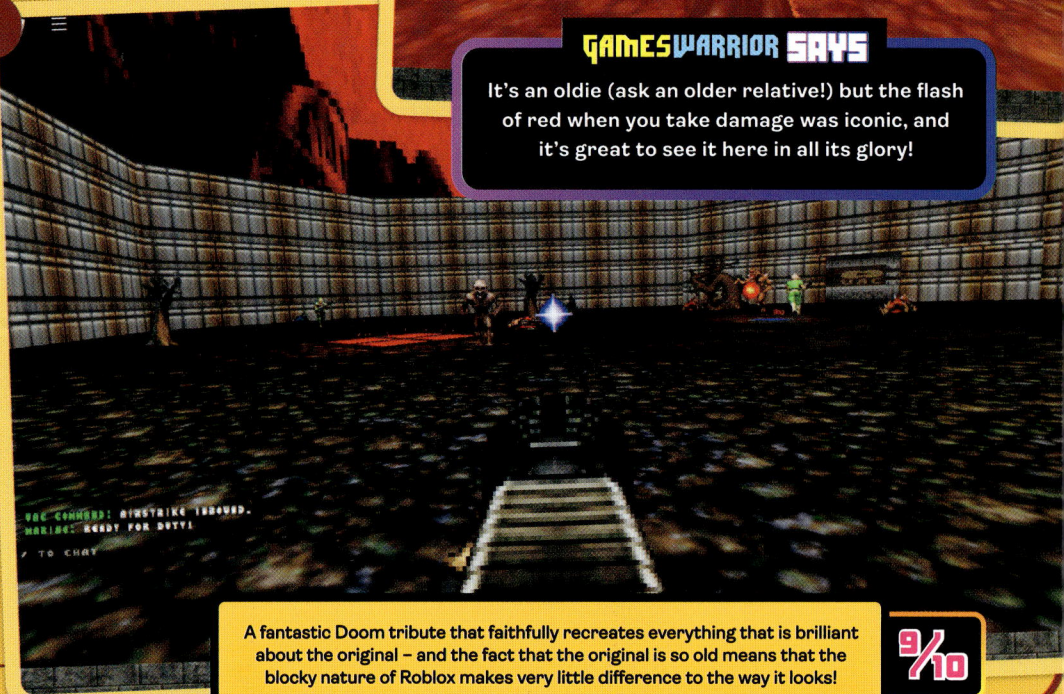

GAMESWARRIOR SAYS

It's an oldie (ask an older relative!) but the flash of red when you take damage was iconic, and it's great to see it here in all its glory!

A fantastic Doom tribute that faithfully recreates everything that is brilliant about the original – and the fact that the original is so old means that the blocky nature of Roblox makes very little difference to the way it looks!

9/10

GAMESWARRIOR VERDICT

STRUCID (FORTNITE)

Strucid is a fast-paced combat and building game that channels the spirit of Fortnite through its dynamic building mechanics and competitive shooting. In this immersive experience, you step onto the battlefield armed with a variety of weapons and the ability to rapidly construct protective structures.

The gameplay in Strucid is all about precision, quick reflexes, and tactical decision-making. As you navigate carefully crafted maps, you engage in intense skirmishes where every second counts. The option to build structures on the fly provides you with a valuable edge, whether you're dodging enemy fire or controlling key areas of the arena. With a diverse arsenal at your disposal, each encounter offers a fresh challenge that tests both your shooting skills and your strategic ingenuity.

BEGINNER'S GUIDE TO ROBLOX STUDIO

Roblox Studio is the tool used to create amazing games and experiences in Roblox. It may seem complicated at first, but once you learn the basics, you'll be able to build anything you can imagine!

1. TEMPLATES

START WITH A READY-MADE WORLD

Before you start building, Roblox Studio gives you different templates to choose from. These are pre-made worlds with different settings, like:

- **Baseplate** – A blank, flat world for full creative control.

- **Village** – A small town to explore and customise.

- **Racing Track** – A road already set up for driving games.

HOW TO USE TEMPLATES:

1. Open Roblox Studio.

2. Click 'New' on the left.

3. Select a template that fits your game idea.

4. Click 'Create', and it will load into the workspace.

Templates help you save time instead of building everything from scratch!

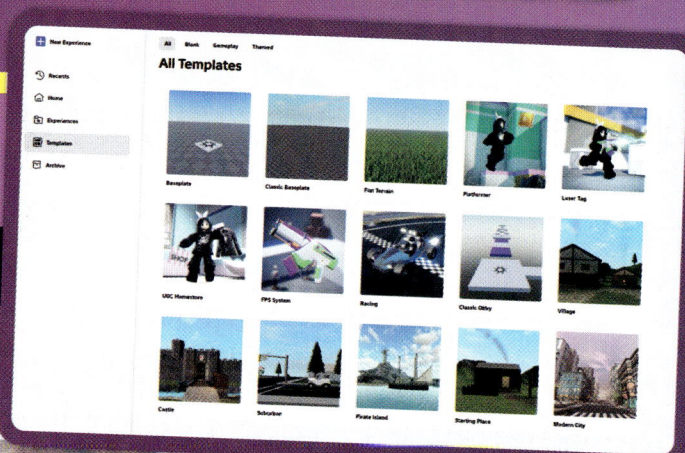

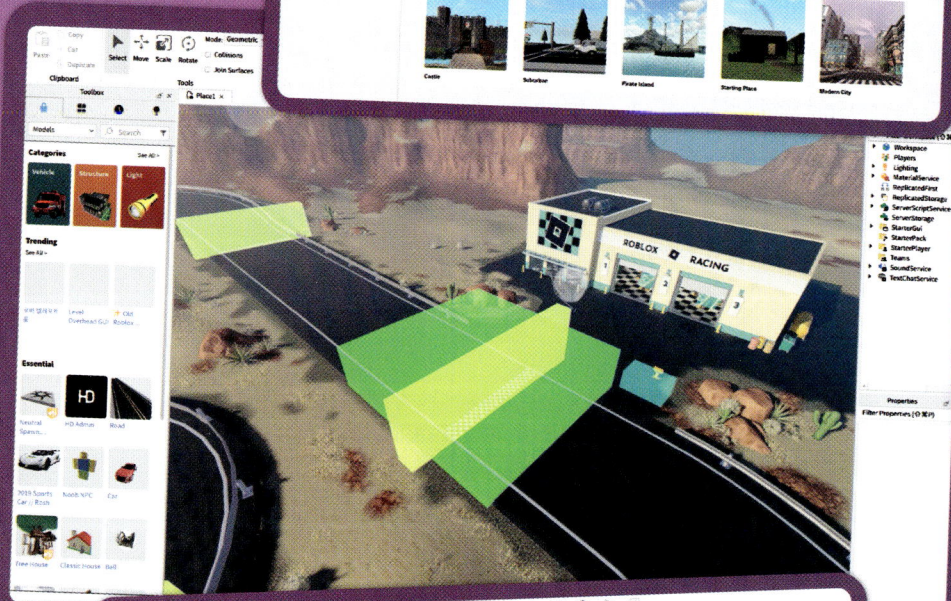

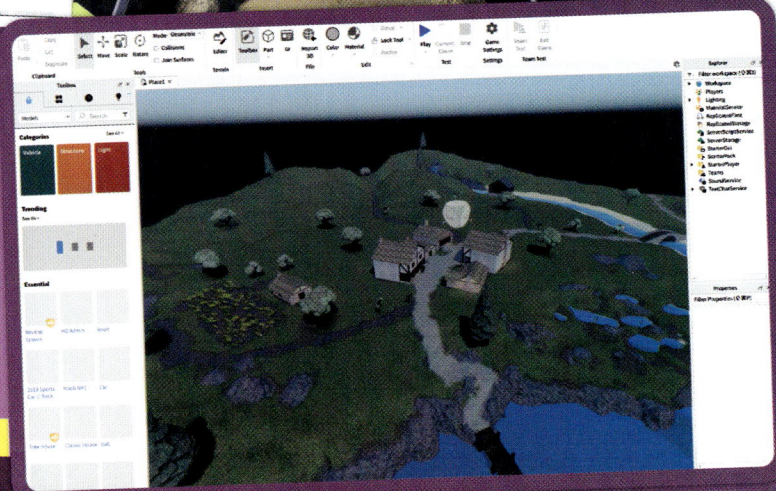

2. TERRAIN

SHAPE YOUR WORLD

Terrain allows you to create realistic landscapes, such as:

- Mountains
- Rivers
- Caves
- Islands

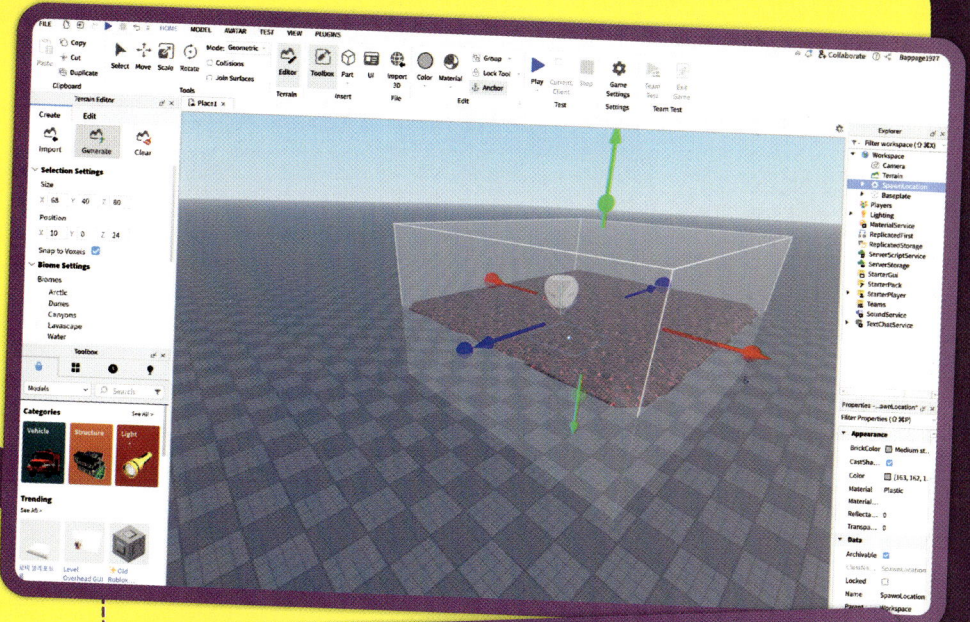

HOW TO USE TERRAIN TOOLS:

1. Go to the Terrain Editor (under "Home" or "Model" tab).

2. **Use different tools to shape the land:**
   - **Generate** – Create new terrain.
   - **Clear** – Remove terrain.
   - **Paint** – Change terrain texture (grass, rock, sand, etc.).
   - **Smooth** – Make terrain look natural.

This is great for making adventure, survival, or open-world games! You can create your world in small, specific stages or you can create one huge area by dragging your cursor then selecting all the different types of terrain you'd like it to involve and Roblox Studio will do the rest! This is a great way to create an island environment in seconds!

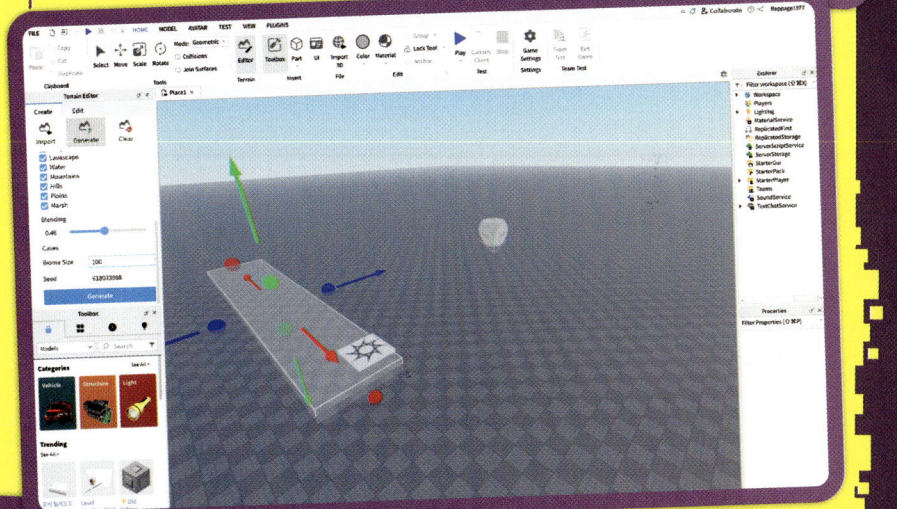

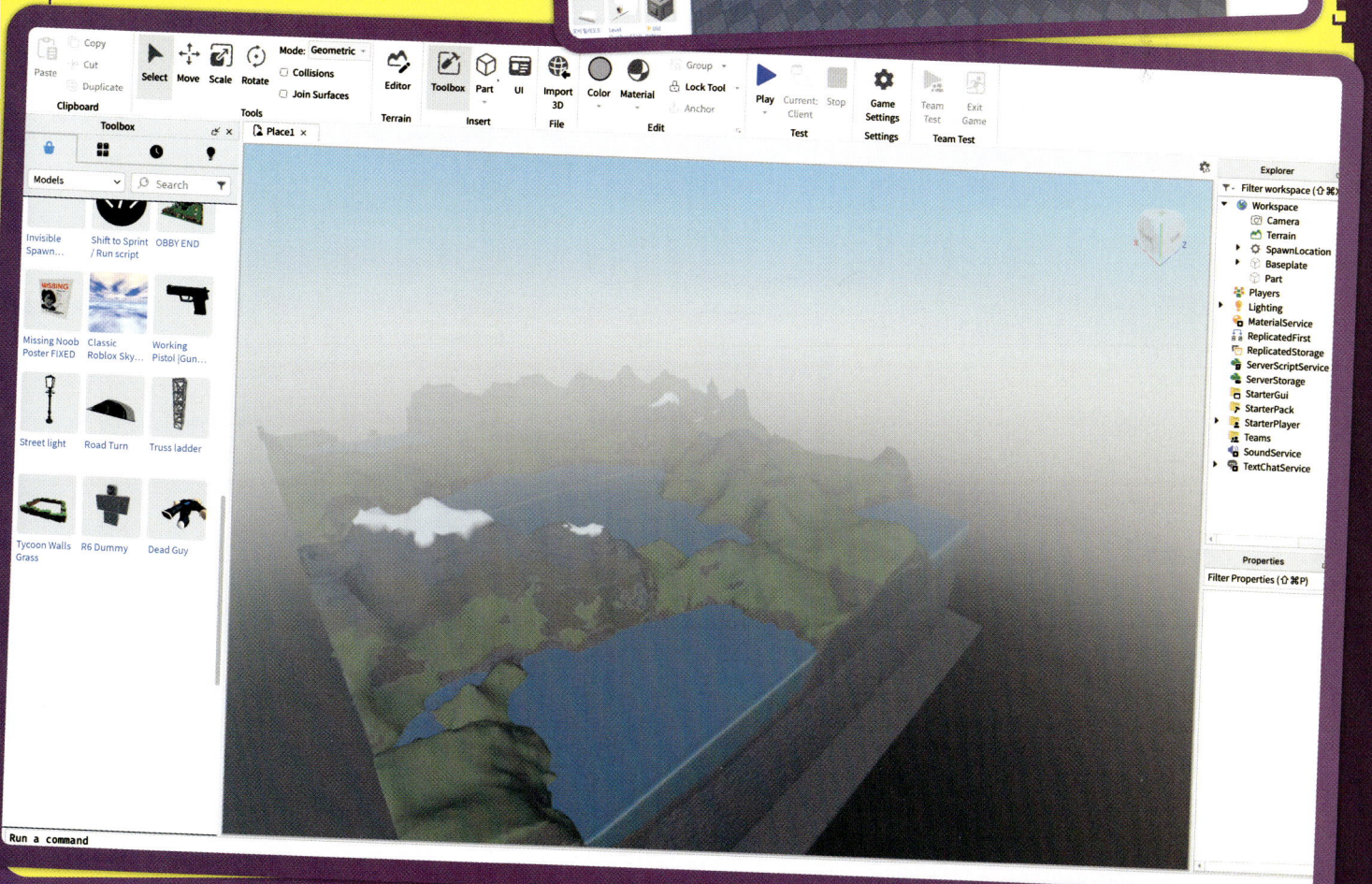

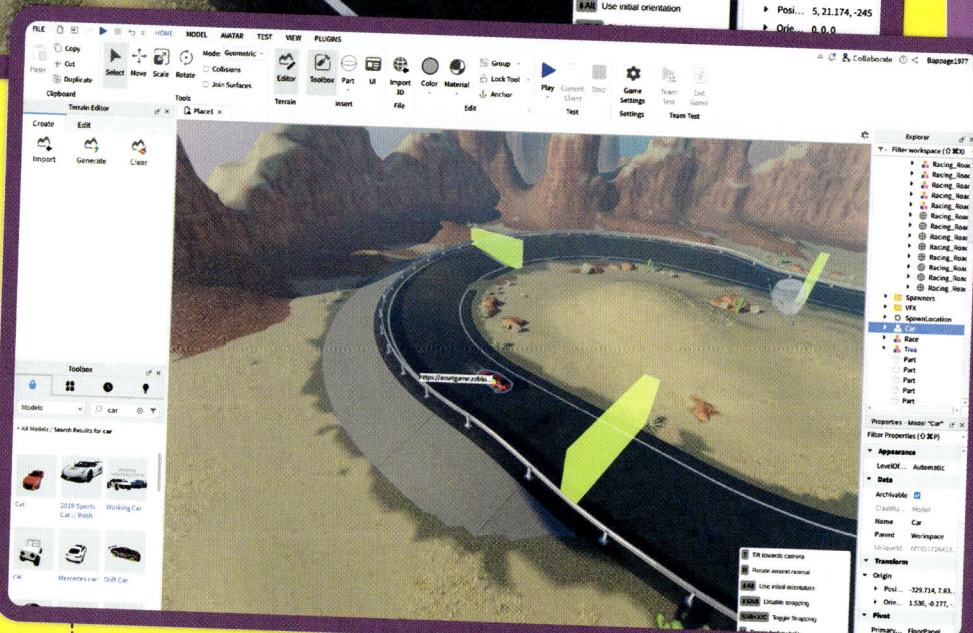

3. PARTS

BUILDING BLOCKS OF YOUR GAME

Everything in Roblox is made of Parts – basic shapes like cubes, spheres, cylinders, and wedges.

HOW TO ADD PARTS:

1. Click on 'Home' tab.

2. Select 'Part' and choose a shape, or select a model from the toolbox.

3. Drag it, resize it, or rotate it to fit your design.

Extra Features:
- **Anchoring** – Stops objects from falling due to gravity.
- **Collision** – Decides whether players can walk through a part or not.
- **Grouping** – Helps organise multiple parts into one object.

By using Parts, you can build anything from houses to spaceships, but they can also help bring your game to life with extra detail!

4. SCRIPTING

ADDING INTERACTIVITY WITH CODE

Scripting makes your game interactive! Laua is the coding language used in Roblox Studio.

Here's a simple script to make a part disappear when touched:

```lua
CopyEdit
script.Parent.Touched:Connect(function()
    script.Parent.Transparency = 1 -- Makes the part invisible
    script.Parent.CanCollide = false -- Players can walk through it
end)
```

HOW TO ADD A SCRIPT:

1. Right-click a Part in the Explorer window.

2. Click 'Insert Object' ↪ 'Script'.

3. Delete the default text and enter your own code.

With scripting, you can create moving platforms, leaderboards and NPCs! Don't worry if it seems like a lot of work though – you can import lots of parts that have pre-written scripts so they will behave as you would expect them to!

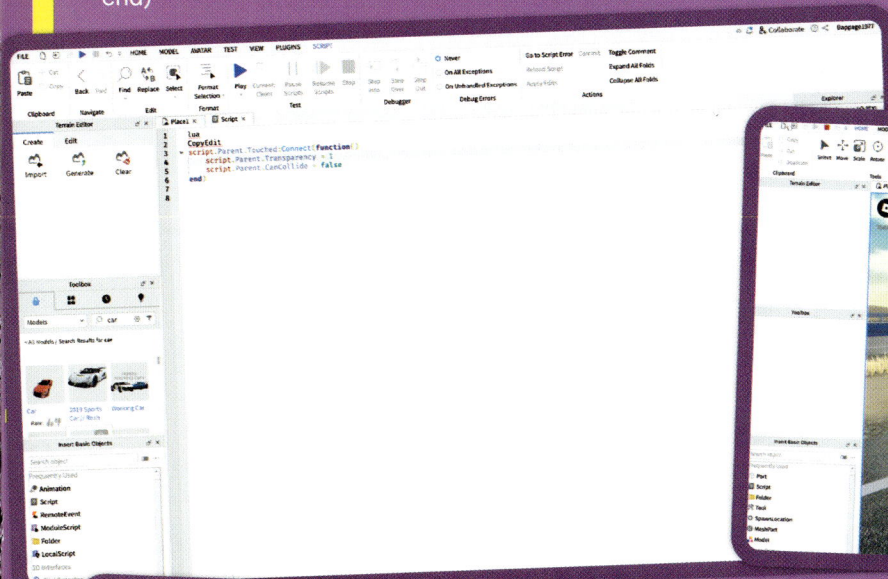

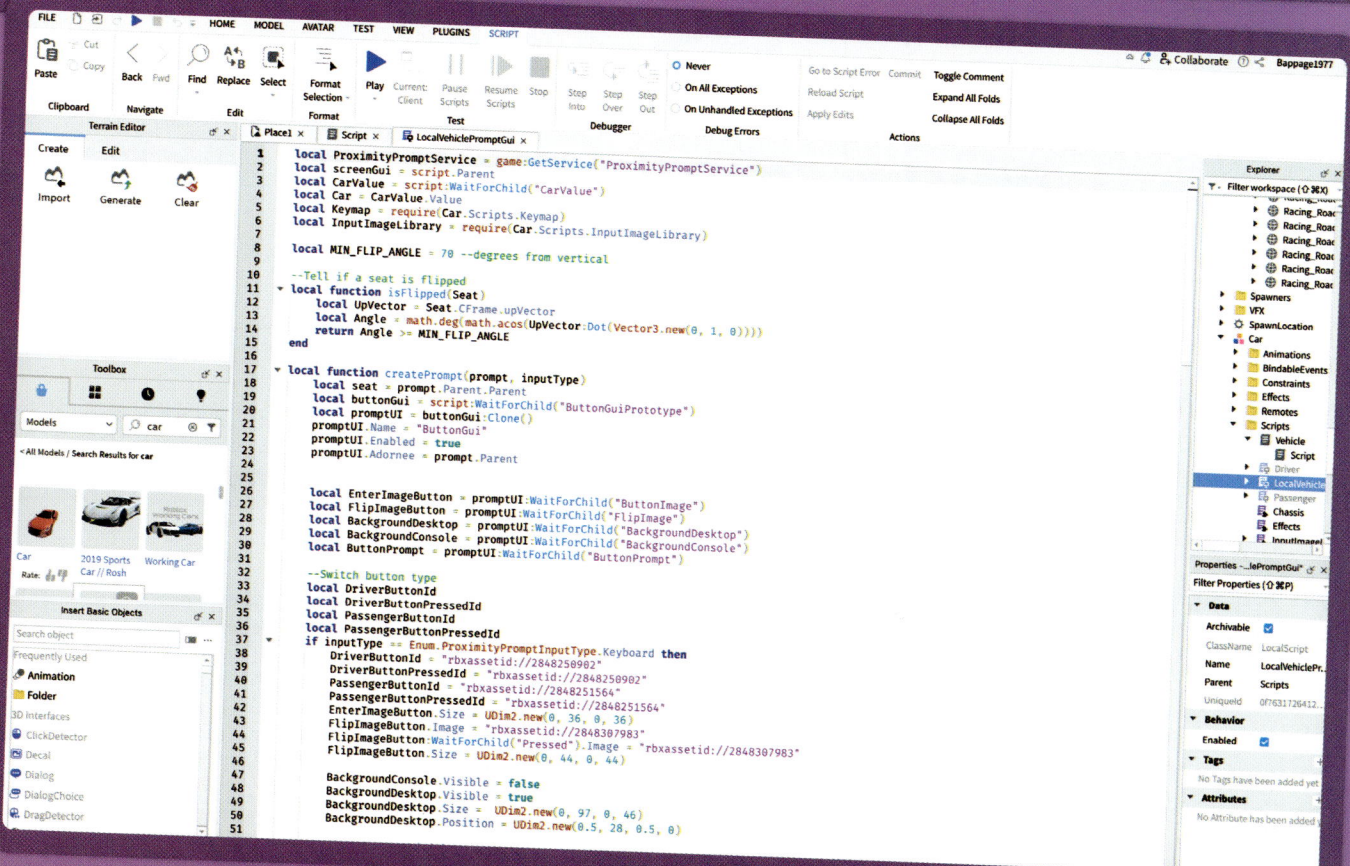

5. LIGHTING AND EFFECTS

MAKING YOUR GAME LOOK AMAZING

Lighting and effects add realism and atmosphere to your game.

Types of lighting:
- **SunRays** – Makes the sun glow.
- **Bloom** – Gives a bright, dreamy effect.
- **Fog** – Creates a mysterious or spooky setting.
- **ColorCorrection** – Changes the overall colour mood (warm, cold, etc.).

HOW TO ADD LIGHTING EFFECTS:

1. Click 'Explorer' (if it's not open, go to View > Explorer).

2. Click the 'Lighting' object.

3. Click 'Insert Object' ↦ Choose a lighting effect.

Lighting helps create the mood of your game, whether it's bright and fun or dark and eerie! You can play with all kinds of settings including contrast to get some really awesome lighting effects!

6. PUBLISHING AND SHARING YOUR GAME

Once your game is ready, you can publish it to Roblox so others can play!

HOW TO PUBLISH YOUR GAME:

1. Click 'File' ↦ 'Publish to Roblox As'.

2. Give your game a cool name and description.

3. Set it to public or private.

4. Click 'Create'!

Now your game is live, and players can join and explore your world!

PUZZLE ANSWERS

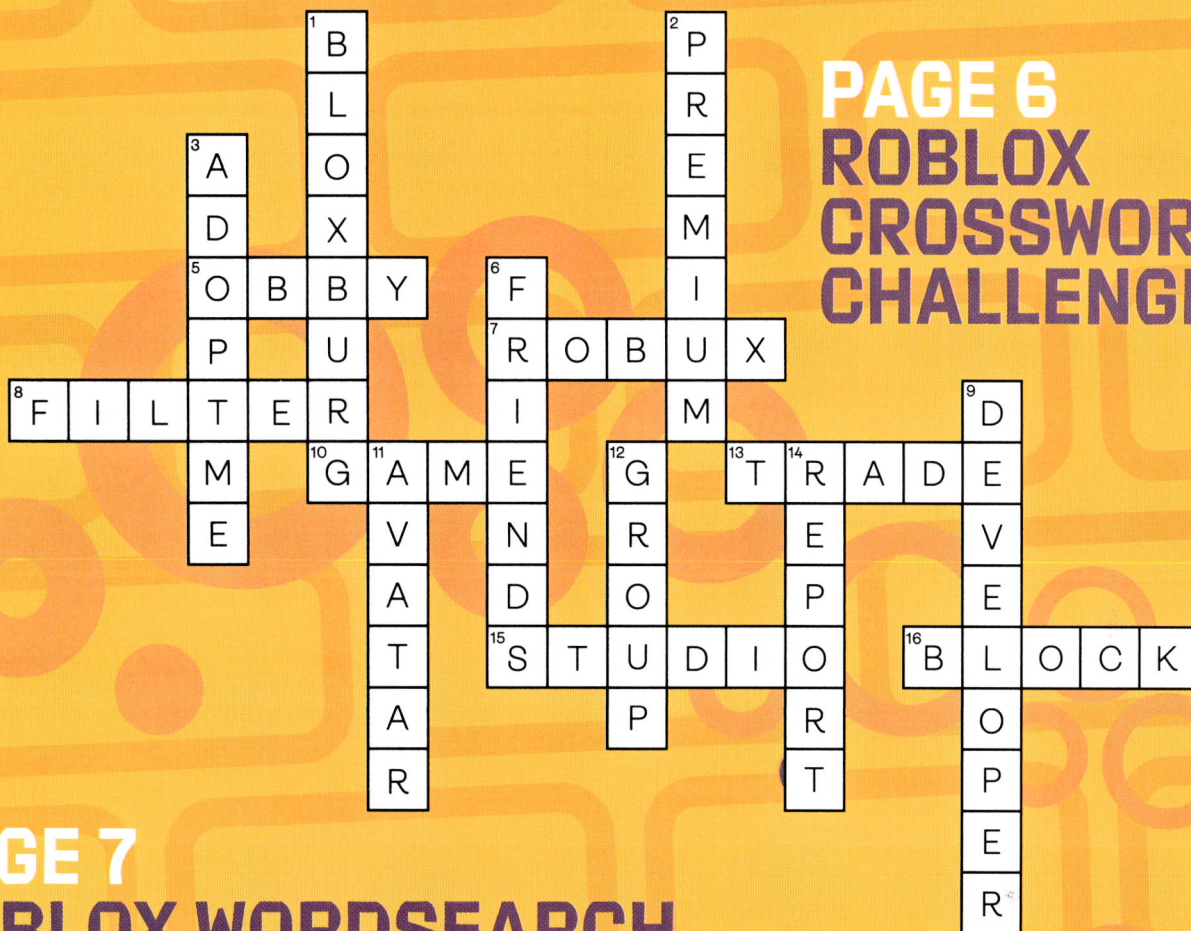

Crossword answers:

1. BLOXBURG (down)
2. PREMIUM (down)
3. ADOPTME (down)
4. OBBY (across)
5. FILTER (across)
6. FIND (down)
7. ROBUX (across)
8. GAME (across)
9. DEVELOPER (down)
10. GROUP (down)
11. AVATAR (down)
12. TRADE (across)
13. REPORT (down)
14. STUDIO (across)
15. BLOCK (across)

PAGE 7
ROBLOX WORDSEARCH CHALLENGE!

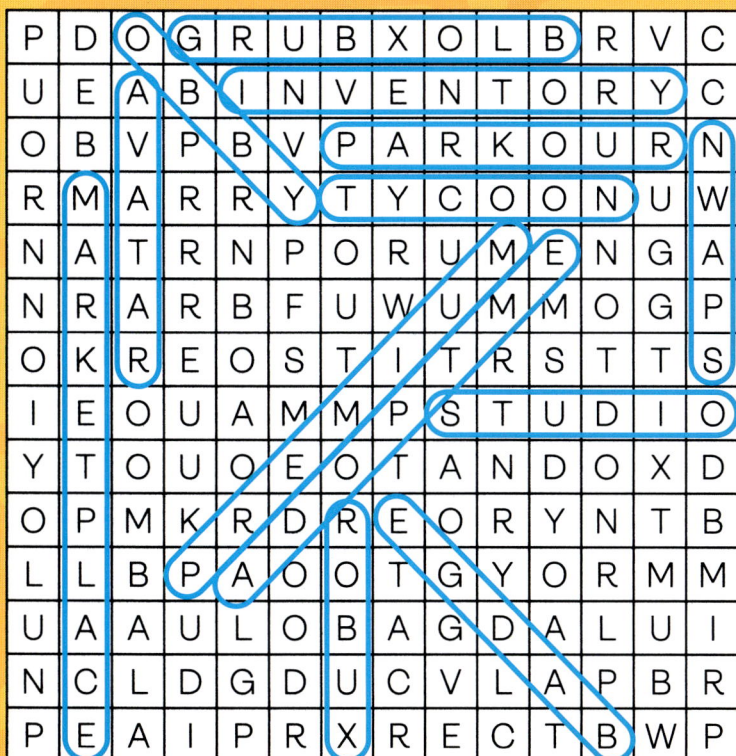

```
P D O G R U B X O L B R V C
U E A B I N V E N T O R Y C
O B V P B V P A R K O U R N
R M A R R Y T Y C O O N U W
N A T R N P O R U M E N G A
N R A R B F U W U M M O G P
O K R E O S T I T R S T T S
I E O U A M M P S T U D I O
Y T O U O E O T A N D O X D
O P M K R D R E O R Y N T B
L L B P A O O T G Y O R M M
U A A U L O B A G D A L U I
N C L D G D U C V L A P B R
P E A I P R X R E C T B W P
```

PAGE 10
ROBLOX QUIZ

1. David Baszuki and Erik Cassel.
2. 2006.
3. Roblox VR.
4. It's an obstacle course.
5. Avatar Editor.
6. Tycoon games.
7. Marketplace.
8. 380 million.
9. Laua.
10. Puzzle games.

77

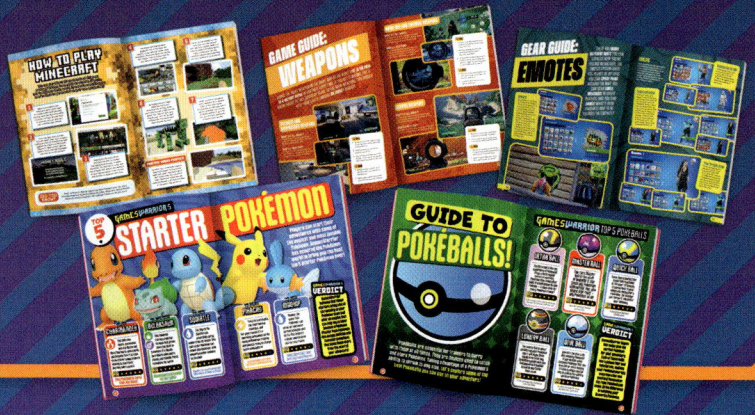

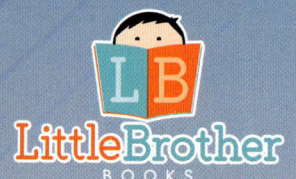